Praise for **FROM**

'An emotional read writte
readers will relate to at leas
An

'We all have a past, and you can either let it define you, or it will be the making of you. Carolyn's story is written from the heart, taking you on a journey of her life. If you have felt anxiety or isolation being in further education away from your loved ones, experiencing teenage pregnancy and don't know where to turn, a full-time mum trying to juggle her studies and home life... Carolyn's book will act like a guiding light for you. A self-help book with plenty of guidance and resources when you don't know what way to turn next.'

Anita Swetman – CEO and published author

'This was such an interesting read. Your warmth shines through from the first page and, although it deals with some really heavy topics, you can see how much you grow (and have grown) as you read each part. Knowing you today, I can see your humour shine through in little snippets and that just shows how far you have come. This is such an important read and it will give hope to so many others out there!'

Molly Paige – primary school teacher

'From a Place Called Shame *written by Carolyn Parker is really anything but shameful. It is an honest account of growing up years before mobile phones and internet* existed. When we could only count on our friends and family. I enjoyed reading this book as it is a book of hope and light. Carolyn is compassionate towards others and has discovered self-development skills to heal her own wounds. It is an honest account of life's ups and downs. It shows how strength of character and positivity can lift up any situation and Carolyn spreads love and light throughout her book, which is a pleasure to read. I highly recommend this book to lift your spirits and restore faith in life.'

Lisa Plutoni – making the world a happier place

'Carolyn writes beautifully about the innocence and naivety that comes with young love in a time when women's choices were limited by circumstance and standing. Her experiences with sexual trauma are handled with gentle sensitivity while mirroring an experience that unfortunately many women can relate to, and the retelling of her termination and subsequent descent into post-traumatic stress and later post-natal depression are heartbreaking.

At every stage of the story, Carolyn demonstrates self-compassion for her younger self, and also for the reader who may be walking a similar path.

From a Place Called Shame is a heartfelt read that shines a light on some of the issues women face alone, and the ripple effects that the heavy weight of this burden creates. A must read.'

Tracey Rampling – CEO of Gemini Moon Press, and Co-Founder of the Women Writing Intentionally Collective

FROM A
PLACE CALLED
SHAME

CAROLYN PARKER

For Kathy
Little did you know how much
your friendship meant to me.
Thank You x

For Tigger
Always remembering your love and support.
With heartfelt thanks.

CONTENTS

INTRODUCTION

We are all human. We all make mistakes, yet some mistakes seem to have an indelible stigma attached to them.

My reason for writing this book is to open a new conversation around what are taboo subjects in many circles and cultures. To reach out to others by sharing my own experience, to create compassionate understanding in those who are spectators and to give encouragement and hope to those for whom these "dirty little secrets", as my father termed them, are a reality in their back story.

It is easy to say you will never be in a situation but what happens when you find yourself in the very place you previously despised?

Looking back, I have greater insight into the dynamics and pressures I experienced at the time and have had the privilege of sitting with my younger self, seeing her pain and inner struggle with fresh eyes.

I know people hold very strong views on these subjects. Everyone has a right to voice their opinion, yet so often we don't appreciate the devastating effect our words can have on those who are hurting in secret.

My aim is to be authentic and tell it as it was, in the hope that others will think again before casting the first stone.

Disclaimer:
Some names in this book have been changed to
protect their identities. The events described are
as the author recalls them, so may not always be
factually accurate. Any errors are the author's. If
you would like to get in touch to correct anything,
please email the author at:
carolyn.parker@restoringselfbelief.co.uk

SHAME

"The intensely painful feeling or experience of believing that we are flawed and therefore unworthy of love and belonging: I am bad."

"I am a mess: The focus is on self, not behaviour, with the result that we feel alone."

Brené Brown

CHAPTER 1

LIFE IN THE COUNTRY

Age 11-18: School Days 1970-1977

Not having brothers or sisters has its benefits. No one telling tales and no competition from noisy siblings jostling for time and attention from their parents. But in other ways it definitely has a downside. There are only so many hours you can happily amuse yourself reading or playing solitaire. Seriously, I became an expert at moving the little red and green pegs of my travel solitaire set until just one remained in the center of the bright yellow plastic board; I even kept a time log detailing numerous attempts to exceed my personal best, such was the need to fill my time once the obligatory homework was completed.

I lived a very sheltered life. The bungalow was set in a third of an acre of ground at the end of a long drive. The only home to be seen from the back terrace was that of a slightly eccentric lady who appeared now and again at our back door with an offering of fresh vegetables. One year, I recall her producing a handknitted, thick cream-and-flecked cardigan with large brown buttons that she had made for me. At first, I didn't take to it, but due to its warmth it became a firm favourite while playing imaginary games with my imaginary friends in the imaginary wood at the bottom of the garden.

A few children lived in the village, just enough to keep the village school open, for a couple of years at least, but I didn't get to know anyone my age until I moved up to the local girls' grammar school and caught the bus five miles into town each day. The nearest neighbour with any children lived opposite the end of my drive, a brother and sister who looked polar opposites in appearance. I was told the boy was adopted and that his sister then made a surprise appearance several years later.

She and I became good friends, out of necessity really, me being six years her senior but longing for a friend to invite to tea and share in my let's-pretend adventures. The big plus was that she had a playroom with a record player, so we got to play all the latest singles and *Top of the Pops* compilation albums at top volume without being shouted at to turn it down! I didn't think much about our age difference at the time, but it meant that I was very naïve about pretty much everything, not having older siblings or friends to pick up the facts of life from or other censored information not mentioned in polite society in my day. You may laugh, as times are very different now, but I had no idea what a boy looked like under his clothes and only a very rudimentary outline as to how babies were made. I can see my biology teacher Miss James now, blushing a dark shade of crimson as she taught the class of third year girls (aged thirteen) the facts of life from a biological point of view and having questions that I didn't even comprehend being fired at her from some of the more mature pupils. I never saw a pornographic magazine and the nearest I got to a steamy novel was a short paragraph in a well-thumbed paperback that was passed round under the chemistry bench when the teacher's back was turned. It featured what we then considered to be a raunchy sex scene in a barn, I recall, but it was very tame by today's standards.

Where am I going with these confessions of a naïve schoolgirl, you may wonder, and you would be right to ask! I'm going to the end of my teen years when there was a party invite every weekend to celebrate the eighteenth birthdays of those in my year or that of the boys' grammar school next door. They were messy affairs, as you can imagine, with plenty of alcohol and testosterone flowing. Separating girls and boys in the week and letting them loose at the weekend was a recipe for mayhem much of the time. Despite there only being the odd whiff of weed around in those days, we still knew how to push the boundaries, resulting in some unfortunate consequences in the way of car and motorbike accidents and the odd unwanted pregnancy.

Anyone – such as my friend Naomi, unfortunate

enough to be in the latter category, was ostracised by the cool crowd and treated by the school as a leper. They were excluded immediately (God forbid that the school's reputation be tarnished) and made to study at home. Should they decide to continue with their exams, they were escorted to a private room away from everyone else and escorted off the premises afterwards. Such was the stigma attached to single mothers in the late seventies in rural Gloucestershire.

Being a late starter, in many ways, I managed to avoid this particular sword of Damocles, only conjuring the wrath of the headmistress for talking on the stairs during examination times, for which I found myself at the dining table writing – by candlelight, due to the power cuts that year – one hundred lines saying: "I must not talk on the stairs during examinations." I didn't incur any further punishments, but in some way it felt exciting, as if I should be writing with a feathered quill and ink pot to hand! I certainly won't forget it!

I met my first long-term boyfriend at one of these school parties. The 10th of December to be exact, in a local cricket club. He was enjoying the camaraderie of his friends with a pint in his hand and I was on the dance floor. I recall him swooping in as a record ended and encircling me with one arm while spilling beer with the other and pulling me gently to the side of the room. It was near the end of the night, soon the lights were on, and people were being encouraged to leave. He asked for my number, but I refused to tell him, saying if he *really* wanted it, he would find it.

The next day was Saturday. I hadn't said anything much about the party to my parents and whiled away the day reading, drawing and walking down the lane to my favourite gate that overlooked a string of fields. A small herd of Friesian cows lived there, and I loved nothing better than to lean on the gate, spending time with my thoughts, unhurried, replaying the night before or what had happened at school, and cogitating, as my father called it. I imagined myself to be a little like Pooh Bear, in *Winnie-the-Pooh*, who would hum a merry tune to himself as he walked or sat on a gate and made up a little ditty that always ended in "tiddley pom"! I am a great fan of the A.A. Milne books, being brought up on them and being given the nickname Piglet by this first "proper" boyfriend, as I called him, who finally found my landline number and called on Saturday afternoon.

I had joined the cool gang overnight, and noticed I was treated with a new level of respect by my classmates, novel for one who often felt a bit of a misfit, being teased for not knowing the meaning of various words of a sexual nature. My social life also took a giant leap forward being invited to all the parties in my year group and his. Apparently, he was well-liked and I was applauded for having landed such a good catch! It was all a fluke from my perspective. I had been plucked off the dance floor without making any conscious decision and had apparently done the best thing ever by playing hard to get. In actual fact, I didn't think he would even remember me, being the wrong side of several pints of beer by that stage in the evening.

My parents were from the stricter side of life, so I was limited initially to only going out on Friday and Saturday evenings and had an eleven o'clock curfew. This is where catching the bus home from school became a godsend. The girls' and boys' grammar schools were next to each other, so you would see a procession of teenage couples walking the mile into town and congregating in the local Wimpy bar for hot chocolate and doughnuts. How I longed for the end of school bell to ring each day and enjoyed the feeling of being accepted as one of the in-crowd. The weekends couldn't come round fast enough, the sixth formers taking over the Berni Inn in town on a Friday and Saturday night or heading to the local halls and other cheap-to-rent venues to celebrate another coming of age with a freely flowing, usually parent run, bar and popular DJ banging out the tunes of the day at top whack until requested to turn the volume down by the nearby irate residents. You could hear the chorus of "Layla" and the strident cords of Deep Purple's "Smoke on the Water" from the end of the street. I was fortunate to have a boyfriend who drove and was a sensible driver, it being his father's car, which reassured my parents, though in hindsight and being a parent myself, I imagine they were always on edge until they heard the back door shut and the key turn in the lock.

The months raced by, my eighteenth party came and went and A levels were upon us before we knew it. Despite being madly in love by this time, I was diligent in completing my homework and revision, as this meant I was allowed out!

The wait for results always seems like an age, doesn't it?

Yet the summer passed by pleasantly enough and I was never happier than when I was with J, whether that was at his house listening to Yes albums while eating Chinese takeaway washed down with a bottle of Blue Nun on a Friday night or walking round the Forest of Dean, sitting on a log for a picnic in a clearing filled with the smell of freshly felled pines.

He really was, as my friends had told me, one of the good guys. I never felt pressured to "rush things", as you might say, and we spent our time just getting to know each other and being really good friends.

Before I knew it, D-day arrived when the A level results were typed up and posted in the window of the senior school side entrance. I was pretty confident I would get the required grades I needed for the physiotherapy school I had chosen in Birmingham. I had only taken two subjects, chemistry and biology, having given up physics after the first term and being made by the headmistress to take the O level instead, tutoring myself! It was a sunny day and there was already a crowd around the lists of names and grades when I arrived. We had arranged to meet up afterwards to hopefully celebrate with our friends in the local hostelry. Sadly, my vision of the day didn't turn out as I had imagined. I needed two Cs to get in, I scraped biology with a D and got an O level grade for chemistry.

In true teen style, I felt as if my world had just collapsed. He too failed to get the grades needed for Aston University to study civil engineering. What were we going to do? Our carefully laid plans to both continue our education in Birmingham disappeared in a flash.

My father worked as a chartered accountant in one of the three remaining wool mills in town, a short distance down a lane opposite my school. I had promised that we would drop in to let him know my results.

I was always a little in awe and slightly scared of my father. He never hurt me and rarely shouted at me, but I still didn't want to get on the wrong side of him. I was literally shaking when I walked up to the reception desk and asked to see him. There were red tear tracks down my face and I guess his secretary forewarned him of my nervous and distressed appearance when she went to tell him of my arrival downstairs. I was embarrassed, I was ashamed; what was I going to say, I wondered, and how would he react? I decided to face him on my own as I didn't want him to turn on J, for it wasn't his fault, nor mine for that matter, as I had revised as best I could over the months leading up to the exams. She called my name and ushered me into Dad's office where he sat, black Bic biro in hand, at a large wooden desk. I blurted out what I guess he had anticipated by my red eyes. I was surprised, maybe due to him being in his work environment, that he wasn't angry as I had imagined he would be. We talked calmly of what I should do next, and it was agreed that I should go straight home to ring the college and inform the principal of my results and then wait to see what she suggested.

NO celebrations for me, then. I caught the next bus home, having wished J good luck for telling his parents and agreeing to meet up later to catch up with each other's plans. Mum was upset; *really* upset. She felt and told me in no uncertain terms that I should have studied harder and gone out less. I nervously rang the college and explained. What happened next was unexpected and truly wonderful. As the principal believed I was the right kind of person for the course, she agreed to waive the entry criteria on this occasion and let me in with my one D grade. What a relief! My frown turned to a smile and the tears to laughter. I was truly grateful to her for seeing my potential and going with her instincts.

J wasn't quite so lucky. He had to ring round the universities that had places left and finally was accepted at Sheffield Polytechnic. We would be separated by some ninety miles. I was concerned what effect this would have on our relationship but determined we would be okay. If it was true love, I reasoned in my romantic way of thinking, something would turn up and all would be well. I shed some tears at the thought, but my fears were partly allayed by the arrival in the porch the morning I was leaving for college of a large parcel. It was a huge teddy bear sporting a pale blue ribbon around its neck and a label made of card referring to me by my nickname, Piglet, assuring me that things would be well from Tigger (his nickname). We already wrote to each other and sent cards before leaving for college, so I stowed all these reminders in a special box to read when I felt lovesick or lonely.

Looking back, I wonder how we ever managed without mobile phones and laptops, without texts and emails and without video calls! We just had letters, cards and landline calls!

CHAPTER 2

AN EXCITING NEW START

Age 18: College Year 1: September 1977

In some ways, I was jealous. There were no freshers' parties at the School of Physiotherapy, but we had some laughs trying on the uniforms we had ordered. The navy trousers were shapeless and polyester, which meant static was a big problem when I forgot to add conditioner to the wash. As for the navy lace-up shoes, they came in a style my grandmother would have worn! The white tunics, however, were smart and gave me a sense of pride after being presented with the college badge to pin on my lapel.

The first weeks were a steep learning curve. Living away from home for the first time was strange yet liberating. The course was structured into lessons similar to a school timetable with homework to complete in the evening. We all lived in the nurses' home on site named after Elizabeth Cadbury, a relative of the famous chocolate-making family. It was a medium-sized, red-bricked, three-storey building within the hospital grounds. I was on the first floor with the other new students. There was a tiny kitchen, a laundry room and two old-fashioned lounges with a TV and armchairs around the perimeter, as you would see in an elderly residential home's sitting room!

I had little knowledge of how to cook and the queue to use the kitchen was always long, so I was very thankful for the hospital canteen and ate there at both lunch and suppertime with a small group of others, quickly resulting in trouser buttons that strained at the waist from too many sausage, egg and chip suppers and treacle pudding with lashings of custard – pure comfort food.

The positive side of this was a chance to forge new friendships, two of which still exist today, a good forty years later.

I thought we would explore Birmingham at the weekend and discover the best nighttime student venues to enjoy life, but much to my amazement I found myself completely alone in the sitting room the first Saturday evening. It turned out that everyone went home or stayed with their boyfriends on weekends. My mum was adamant I couldn't come home for at least six weeks to get over any home sickness and J was living in digs near the Sheffield Wednesday ground that didn't allow girlfriends to stay, so I felt very alone and cheated in some way. I had looked forward to a live and active social life but there was none, nothing at all, except for the termly nurses' home disco, which wasn't much to write home about.

Occasionally, a couple of others would stay over and we would venture to the university bar, but this was a rare occurrence. However, one such outing ended up with me getting into a rather tricky situation. My friends wanted to leave early as it was a cold, snowy December evening. I wanted to stay. I was enjoying the opportunity to have a bop to the tunes of the day, I'd met a medical student who I was getting on well with and he said he'd walk me home. Warning bells were going off in my mind, but I discounted them, having had a few too many rum and cokes and enjoying this rare night out.

When the time came for us to leave, he started to walk me home, taking a route away from the main road through the university campus. We were going in roughly the right direction, so I didn't panic. After about half an hour or so, we reached his men's only residence. He said he needed the toilet and asked me to come in for a coffee.

I can hear you screaming at me now, but in my naivety, I took him at his word and thought he meant a coffee. Once inside, it felt welcoming and warm compared to the icy winter wind outside. He made us both a coffee and we chatted and listened to music, sitting on the floor of his bedsit. He told me we needed to keep our voices down as he wasn't allowed girls in his room. It was getting to the early hours of the morning, and I wanted to leave and go back to my residential block, but I was afraid to go on my own and he had no intention of going with me. I felt trapped. The door was locked, I wasn't allowed to even be there, and he wanted to go to bed. I talked for as long as I could to stay *out* of the bed, but I couldn't put it off forever and I was really tired. I turned my back towards him to face the wall in his cramped single bed. He just lay there, holding me, obviously aroused as I tried to ignore him and go to sleep.

Sleep was impossible. I kept thinking how to get through the night and out of the room and feeling particularly foolish as I loved my boyfriend and hadn't wanted to be in this guy's room, let alone in his bed. Finally, I gave in to his desires, thinking he would leave me alone afterwards if I did. I literally lay back with my eyes closed and thought of England.

Early in the morning, only a couple of hours later, he escorted me off the premises. I couldn't wait to get back to my room, to a safe place.

Each floor had a toilet, wash basin and shower block plus a single bathroom with a large, old-school, white enamel bath. I ran the deepest, hottest, bubbliest bath and soaked in there as long as I could to remove the scent of his body, his sheets, his room. Yet despite scrubbing myself all over with the bath brush, I still felt unclean and dirty somehow.

I reasoned it was my fault. I shouldn't have stayed out on my own, I should have realised I was in danger and not accepted his invitation to go inside and I should have held out longer and not given in to him.

How would I tell J what had happened? How would he react? I loved him so much and I was *so* scared he would finish with me as a result of this one night of stupidity on my part. The rest of the week I was upset and worried.

That Friday, being the start of the Christmas holidays, I bought a coach ticket home. It was the cheapest way to travel. I was met by my mum in the car at Cheltenham Coach Station. It was a joy to be surrounded by home comforts and I relished the wholesome cooking and chatting away to her about what I'd learnt that term. She had a keen interest in human biology and listened intently to me as I demonstrated the names and locations of all the ridges and bumps on the human skeleton and told her all about the treatments I had been perfecting. She particularly enjoyed my massage skills, which I practised on her back and legs.

J was also home, as were all our university friends during the Christmas break. There was much to catch up on over a few noisy pints, but I also managed some alone time with him at his home, striding across the railway bridge and up the hill behind their house, with Robbie-dog, the friendly Border Collie.

I broached the difficult subject of the night of the university disco with tears and apologies and, although obviously upset with me at what had occurred, I was forgiven.

Interestingly, he didn't mention the word rape and I didn't realise it was until very much later in my life when the event came to mind during a counselling session.

The holidays were over far too quickly, as holidays always are. Spring term brought mock first-year exams and practice vivas. These were practical/aural exams, and very nerve-racking as almost any subject could come up. I passed with flying colours.

The summer term rushed past. I spent every free second in the college library researching and writing up my project, "Understanding the Aetiology and Treatment of Osteoarthritis in the Hip Joint", or revising. My files went everywhere with me, including on the coach trip home for half term.

I looked forward to the break times in my revision timetable and the odd day out with J for a walk at a nearby lake at Chew Magna (wonderful name) or in the Forest of Dean.

We both passed our first-year exams and were glad of some lazy summer days at home. I spent most of mine longing for him to call to arrange a time to pick me up. We usually went to his house where I always felt accepted and welcomed. His mum was a social worker, so I felt an affinity towards her straight away and chatted happily about my course. She cooked the best teas, my favourite being chicken marengo, with delicious puddings and cheese for afters. J's dad made home-brewed beer and wine and a bottle of elderberry often accompanied the meal. Many happy times were had under that roof, and I will always be grateful for the way they treated me as part of the family.

CHAPTER 3

BIRMINGHAM

Age 19: College Year 2: September 1978

Have you ever noticed that the start of a new venture and the last sprint to the finish line are exciting and fuelled by motivational energy, yet the period in the middle feels like wading through quicksand or thick black treacle?

Having breezed through year one, it gave me quite a shock. I was now in college in the morning and travelled to local hospital placements on a rota basis in the afternoon. It was exciting but daunting being on the coal face as a very new student, and I was treated in a variety of ways. At best, I was encouraged and taught clinical skills, being allowed to practise my newfound knowledge in a supervised setting. At worst, I was treated as a nuisance and basically did little other than watch from a distance with minimal interaction, except to make the tea for the staff. The workload that year increased considerably, with additional homework and a book of CARBs to complete. CARBs weren't anything to do with food. The acronym stood for Continual Assessment Record Book and consisted of about forty-nine practical assessments, varying from exercise class planning and execution to the use of faradism to stimulate and re-educate the intrinsic muscles of the foot in the case of dropped arches and everything in between. We were even trained in the use of a microwave machine, a new heat treatment, later outlawed due to the effect it had on the therapist's reproductive organs! I digress. I had to pass all forty-nine to qualify before the final exams in the summer of year three.

As an additional pressure, everyone had to move out of the accommodation block on site from the end of year one. This meant groups of students getting together and searching for accommodation in the local paper's small ads section, shop and university noticeboards, and by word of mouth. Google hadn't been born and mobiles didn't exist, which made finding accommodation to rent along with competition from Birmingham and Aston University students quite a task.

I found myself in a limbo situation. My best friend was asked to share with three other students, which left me out in the cold. I approached another set of three friends and was accepted to be the fourth to share a large ground floor Victorian terrace flat in Moseley, two bus rides from college.

It meant sharing a room, which would have been

fine, but sadly, despite my best efforts, it didn't work out well. Being so large and not having central heating, it was like living in a glacier in the winter, ice coating the inside, as well as the outside of the single-thickness windowpanes. The living room had a high ceiling with one small gas fire. We crowded around this to warm our legs, but it was very inefficient and didn't reach our backs. Consequently, any washing on the clothes horse at the end of the room took days to dry and no one dared to use the bath or washroom apart from a quick hand wash or brush of their teeth. We did wash, just not in the house, getting up extra early to use the college showers before lessons began.

Anyone living in Birmingham will know that buses rarely travel on time, or individually; they mostly travel in convoy, and they grind to a halt when it snows. I would be at the bus stop waiting for my ride along the Bristol Road to appear on the horizon, nervously checking my watch, when three would appear. Only the first would stop, the others overtaking it. In the morning rush, this was a nightmare, as at times the first bus only had one or two seats left that were taken by those ahead of me in the queue and I would be left stranded for a further twenty minutes before another caravan of buses would approach. Maybe things have improved in the last forty years. For the sake of the users of public transport today in the West Midlands, I sincerely hope so.

If I was hoping that my living conditions would

evoke a degree of sympathy from my mother, then I was mistaken. In fact, the reaction I received was quite the opposite. She thought living out would toughen me up. Mum regularly regaled me with boarding school tales of waking to an iced flannel over the water jug and Jack Frost patterns on the bedroom window. In her view, this experience would teach me the value of money and help me appreciate the luxury of running hot water and central heating in the future. Sadly, she wasn't able to see the effect it was having on my mental and emotional health.

I felt left out and lonely much of the time and lived for the weekends. Thursday evening would find me packing my navy-blue multi-pocketed overnight bag in preparation for my weekend escape. I can recall the excitement and happiness I felt as I hung up my uniform at four o'clock and pulled on my jeans, anticipating the familiar train journey from Birmingham New Street via Derby and Chesterfield with the crooked spire, up to Sheffield. When my work placement was at Broad Street outpatient department, I would catch the early train if I was lucky. Living in a time before the invention of home computers or the internet, there were no pre-booked tickets and it was the luck of the draw as to whether I chose a fast moving queue at the ticket office.

Once safely seated on the Intercity 125, at a table if possible, facing the direction of travel preferably (I've never liked travelling backwards), I would smile inwardly and outwardly, get out some work to do on the journey, and picture J waiting for me at the entrance to Sheffield Station. The journey was just long enough for me to complete my weekly college assignments or a good chunk of them, and just short enough to enjoy without developing numbness in my gluteal muscles.

As the weeks passed by, I became an expert in recognising the final approach to the station. The carriages usually came to a gentle halt adjacent to the wide central staircase. There was always a rush along the platform through a sea of bodies and bags of varying sizes to the stairs, which led up to the bridge across the tracks with another flight of metal stairs leading down to the exit. As I crossed the bridge, I would peep through the railings to see if J was among the small crowd of people waiting for friends or relatives below. My heart would skip a beat if I spotted him.

This was my weekly routine throughout the year, apart from in the holidays, of course, when we both returned to leafy Gloucestershire.

J had been fortunate to get on a list of students to share a student house with three others in an area referred to as Norfolk Park. It was basic but modern with an open-plan kitchen/lounge area. His room was downstairs, and visitors were allowed.

Weekends had a familiar pattern to them. Friday and Saturday evenings were disco nights at the polytechnic's students' union building. At last, I had the regular social life I craved. I would dance the night away, chatting to his friends and their girlfriends before becoming aware of how sore my feet were as I hobbled back up the hill, via the chip butty van if I was lucky, to Norfolk Park. That hill always seemed so much longer and steeper on the way home; and being a bit tipsy, I guess I was taking a zigzag route. I often took my shoes off, but I'm not sure if that made it any more comfortable to walk.

Why is it that I always seemed to wake up partway through the night, freezing cold, with my back against the wall and no sign of his single quilt anywhere near me?

Saturday mornings were lazy, late affairs with the faint aroma of a cooked breakfast in the kitchen above encouraging us to get up. There's nothing like a fry up to set you up for the day after the night before and I must admit all the guys seemed very able at cooking a delicious mound of eggs, bacon, sausage and tomato with toast and a mug of steaming hot tea to wash it down. Thus fortified, we usually hit the city centre shops, as I was keen to find jeans or tops, trainers or sandals most weeks. Looking back, I realise just how patient J was, waiting for me to try on a myriad of outfits every weekend.

Saturday and Sunday afternoons were often spent at the local park in the summer, strolling, sitting, lying on the grass to soak up the sun or enjoying an ice cream from the van parked at the entrance. So many simple, happy memories were made doing very little and just chilling, as my younger friends would put it.

I've always had a tussle to keep my weight down and, with this in mind, I suggested we booked a polytechnic squash court for a Sunday morning game. I was a complete novice but with a bit of instruction and a lot of practice I started to really enjoy it. My best stroke was to bounce the ball off the front and back wall to drop dead at the back corner of the court so it couldn't be returned. After a good workout, we would retire to the local pub for a shandy or beer to rehydrate and mull over the finer points of the game. You can probably tell that these weekends were the lifeblood of my college days, mainly filled with happiness and love. There were the odd arguments, but my memory hasn't held onto those.

I found the last hour before my train to return to Birmingham the hardest. We often had a burger and chocolate fudge cake with cream at a little burger bar near the squash club en route to the station. The goodbye hugs and "I love yous" were always difficult. I just didn't want to let go and go back, and I would usually dissolve into embarrassed tears as the train rolled out of the station with my face pressed to the window until I lost sight of J on the platform.

Such is love!

My world was this mix of happy loved-up weekends and challenging learning curve weeks with deadlines and new skills to meet and master. Generally, all was well with my soul.

Every other day I would find a white manilla envelope addressed to me, with the other student post laid out in alphabetical order on the top of a large chest of drawers just inside the front door of the college building. This would contain a sheet or two of lined A4 filing paper filled with J's latest news, ink pen sketches of Tigger and Piglet on "an adventure" and reassurances that he missed me and was looking forward to the next weekend together. I kept them for many years and, when I felt lonesome, I would reread them and feel the warmth of his love reaching out to me. I wrote back as soon as I could and I wonder now how I found news and words to fill these missives as we also spoke on the one and only pay phone several times a week.

Then suddenly my life changed.

CHAPTER 4

ALL WASN'T AS IT SEEMED

Age 19: College year 2: January 1979

That winter was harsh. Living with flatmates that weren't really mates was rough and made me feel unwanted. Living in a cold, Victorian-style, ground-floor flat with high ceilings, single-pane sash windows, high ceilings that sucked the heat away from the one tiny gas fire was tough and meant I was always cold and, with it, miserable. Living two bus rides away from college and waiting for ages at Birmingham city bus stops in the bitter wind with icy rain or snow blowing in my face was demoralising. Attacked on all sides, my usual cheeriness and love of life started to show a few cracks. If it hadn't been for the lure of the weekends in a lovely warm student house with good company and ample free food, I may well have quit my course altogether. My initial enthusiasm had dwindled, and the finish line seemed miles away. I recall having the "what if" conversation with my mum one day. What if I left college? What else would I like to do? What else could I do? She had trained in domestic science, and I had shown promise in the subject at school, so possibly I could train in catering? My heart wasn't really in it, though, and we didn't speak of it again.

Then life took a turn that forced us all to reassess where I was and what the future held. I started to feel rather unwell, typically feeling nauseous at coffee time, but this was usually corrected with a cup of tea served by the friendly tea lady in white china teacups and a snack-sized pack of bourbon, shortcake or custard cream biscuits. Every day I tried to be disciplined and walk past them but most days I gave in. I swear cakes and biscuits are magnetised to me, they have always seemed to jump into my hand despite my not-so-valiant attempts to stop them. Will power has always been a challenge when it comes to sweet things.

Apart from these occasional bouts of queasiness, which I put down to my poor diet and tendency to buy food from the reduced shelf of the bargain mini mart that was close to its use-by date to save as many pennies as possible for my weekend adventures up north, I felt pretty well. It would pass, I was sure of that. However, no matter how much I tried to ignore it, I continued to feel rather bloated and under the weather as the weeks went by.

We had a college doctor, a kindly lady who I will call Dr B, who held a lunchtime surgery in a small room of the main hospital the college was linked to once a week. I made an appointment to see her, expecting her to tell me I had a bout of food poisoning. I sat down and told her how I'd been feeling the last month or so. She asked some basic questions about my bowel habits and frequency of the sicky feeling, which I'd expected. Then she leant forward a little, in a manner doctors do when they have bad news to impart, and asked a question that totally stunned me.

"Is there any chance you may be pregnant?" she said.

The question hung in the air as if she'd typed the words on a manual typewriter and left that one sentence on a blank sheet of paper for all to see.

I wanted them to be unsaid, to rewind the film to the moment before she spoke, for to do so would restore my inner peace.

I felt shocked and stupidly naïve at the same time. I was nineteen, yet I honestly hadn't considered this option. I felt betrayed by my friends who had known of the increasing nausea and never suggested this possibility to me. Why hadn't they taken me to one side and kindly mentioned their suspicions?

Writing this in 2021 it seems an impossible scenario for a teenage girl not to be aware of the symptoms of early pregnancy, yet here I was with a look of disbelief and surprise on my face, contemplating the possibility that I might be pregnant.

I replied that it was possible, but that my periods

were three months or more apart, so I hadn't thought anything of not having had one in a while. That was the truth, it was normal for me. It was hard to recall the exact date of my last period, but it had to be about a couple of months. The enormity of the situation suddenly hit me. If this was the case, if Dr B was correct, if I was pregnant, I had very little time to play with, very little time to take it in and even less time to weigh up the stark options that would lie ahead of me.

There was just a possibility. I might *not* be pregnant, it might still be a stomach issue, the doctor just needed to say it, to rule it out, I justified.

The rest of the consultation is a blur. The question was on repeat in my head. "Is there a chance you may be pregnant?" Those eight words would haunt me for years to come. I was given a specimen tube and requested to take a urine sample first thing the next morning and to drop it into her surgery a few miles away, on my way into college. Luckily, it was on my usual bus route, so I made an excuse to my flatmates to leave half an hour before them to catch the early bus. Thankfully the buses that day were all running on time and my plan to jump off, drop the sample in and catch the next bus up to college before they appeared worked out well. I have no idea what classes I had that day, but I know I stayed on site in the afternoon, as I recall the gut-wrenching bus journey to her surgery to get my results in person.

My palms were sweaty with anxiety and my heart

racing. In those days, you just turned up at a doctor's surgery and sat on hard, dark wooden chairs around the perimeter of the waiting room and were seen in turn, unless an emergency case arrived, in which case they took precedence over those in the queue. That wait seemed one of the longest I have experienced in my whole life. The room was almost full when I arrived. I picked up a well-thumbed magazine from a square table, which had seen better days, in the middle of the space and took a seat. Being interested in people, I surveyed those waiting; a motley collection, mostly middle-aged with a couple of harassed mothers of young children for whom waiting quietly didn't come naturally. I wondered what brought them to the doctor. Was it the runny nose and persistent cough, or maybe earache or not eating? Periodically, my brain would remind me that I may be carrying a child of my own inside me and that thought would set off a spike of anxiety that I felt as a tightness in my shoulders and inside my stomach. Slowly, we moved round the room in a solemn ceremony akin to musical chairs without the music. One coming out of the consultation room, one getting up to go in, the rest of us moving round to the next chair and resettling ourselves until the next time we heard the door open, and the game was repeated.

I scanned the magazine I had chosen from the middle of the pile. I just looked at the headlines and the pictures, really, as I couldn't concentrate enough to read. I tried, but found I was reading the first sentence over and over and still not taking it in. Such were my nerves as I waited to hear my fate. The moving round the room game I imagined to be like climbing up a roller coaster, the anxiety and anticipation of the ride building as you headed up, up, up to the point of no return. It lulled me into a false sense of security as I assumed I would continue around until I was adjacent to the doctor's room and therefore next to be seen.

Just as I started to relax a little, the door opened and Dr B's head popped out. I thought she was wanting to catch the receptionist's eye for something, but I was wrong. She scanned the room, caught *my* eye and announced my name, holding the door ajar for me, as I nervously picked up my bag and dropped the magazine back on the top of the pile. This was it. I would walk into that room not knowing and walk out with a definite answer to the question: "Am I pregnant?"

CHAPTER 5

A VERY BIG QUESTION ANSWERED

Still aged 19: College Year 2: February 1979

I sat down and waited for Dr B to take her seat at the other side of the desk. I wonder how many times a year, or in her professional life she has faced this particular conversation. I wonder what her personal feelings were about it and whether this has ever had an impact on her own family. I wonder how she learnt to be emotionally detached when faced with a teenage girl sitting across from her desk awaiting her pronouncement as to her condition.

You would imagine this pivotal moment would be etched in my mind, yet try as I might, I can't recall the doctor's voice or exact words. There's just an image of my younger self seated, waiting, and of that same younger self walking to my friend's house afterwards.

The conversation that occurred between these two events was the most pivotal exchange of words in my life thus far, yet my brain has failed to retain them. In essence, she told me my result was positive, I was pregnant and as this was starting to permeate my mind and emotions, she seemed to suggest that to contemplate getting married and having the child wasn't in my best interests. I recall feeling somewhat surprised at this but understood that such a reason to settle down in the late seventies wasn't the best and may well have ended up in disaster, and that my boyfriend and I were halfway through further education courses that would see us both achieving a good level of education with jobs to go to. I was given an appointment for the city BPAS (British Pregnancy Advisory Service) centre for the following week and walked out in a daze. I wonder, if I could have read the minds of those still waiting to be seen, what their thoughts were that day. Had they guessed the situation or thought I had been told some other equally disturbing news?

I walked to the shared terraced house where my best friend Kathy was living with three others in my college year. I hoped she was in. I wasn't sure what her response to the news I was about to share would be, as she was part of the Christian Union, which was headed up by a fiercely evangelical Canadian mature student in my year group. I was allowed round the back door as I was a friend and could smell the welcoming waft of supper cooking as I neared it. I was surprised to find all four housemates in the kitchen preparing savoury mince. It smelt delicious but my stomach lurched a little at the fatty aroma. They were always very welcoming and were used to me turning up unannounced, happily sharing whatever food they had with me, and I often wished that I'd been able to house share with them. I know I would have enjoyed it far more than my current lodgings. The house was a short bus journey away from college and, being in the middle of Selly Oak, was close to all the local amenities, including a hospital where many of my placements were scheduled.

They quickly noticed I wasn't my usual chatty self and asked what the matter was. I asked to talk to Kathy on her own for a minute and, cup of tea in hand, followed her into the downstairs bedroom she shared with another Cathy.

I sat at the end of her bed and told her the whole sorry story. All credit to her, she didn't say anything judgmental; I will always be thankful for that. She was loving and kind and compassionate towards me. She listened and held space for me, allowing me to let the words tumble out until there were no more. She provided tissues while I cried and blew my nose and felt a complete mess inside and out. She never turned her back on me, not then, not ever, which meant more than any words can ever say. She also kept it to herself. One of my worst fears was that the news would quickly travel around the whole college, and I would be given withering looks or be shunned by the rest of my year group, as Naomi had been at school.

We chatted a while and then she prayed with me for peace, courage and the wisdom I needed in my decision making. She was and will always be a true friend. In fact, I have dedicated this book to her in gratitude for her loving kindness towards me.

I didn't want to go "home" that night. Kathy shared her evening meal of mince, potatoes and carrots with me, and I watched TV with everyone in the front room. I was among friends. Having slept overnight on the sofa, we set off to college together in the morning. My afternoon placement was a few streets away from my rental flat, so it was easy to drop in afterwards, get changed and pick up my weekend bag before heading to the station.

In one way, I couldn't wait to be with J again, to feel the warmth and safety of his student house, be around friends and to feel him holding me close and secure. In another way, I was very nervous. Everything was so different now. This time I had to tell him I was pregnant with his baby. This time I felt uncertain and scared of his reaction. Would he reject me and end our relationship? Would he even believe it was his? Would he listen and accept his side of the responsibility for my situation? I hoped he would, but I didn't know for sure, and this was causing a cascade of butterflies in my stomach on top of the waves of nausea that seemed to last most of the day now.

The actual moment of sharing this momentous news has strangely been erased from my memory, but I do know that I was in his bedroom getting changed ready to go out for the evening. I had made a pinafore-style dress out of a beautiful length of sea-blue fabric from Laura Ashley. It was more expensive than the average cotton material I bought to sew up a variety of evening tops on Mum's old Singer sewing machine. This was a warmer weave with a tie round the back and balloon-style long sleeves. It was the fashion of the day and luckily its loose-fitting style was perfect to hide my slightly extended stomach. I wore it with knee-length tan leather boots. They had three-inch broad heels, so felt both stylish and comfortable.

I know I cried when I told him. I know he didn't shout at me and that he didn't say we needed to split up. In fact, we had bought tickets the previous week to an Alan Ayckbourn play showing at the Crucible Theatre, so had somewhere specific to go that evening, which helped the conversation along. I found it hard to concentrate on the play, as you can imagine, but have a vivid recollection of the interval. As many theatres do, we had ordered interval drinks before the performance. I stood in the bar holding a cup of coffee and was having distinctly warm feelings of being a little family. The thought that no one around us knew of the existence of this unborn life strangely filled me with a sense of pride and excitement; it was as if I was practising how it felt to be an expectant mum, pushing away the decision that had almost been made for me by the doctor only two days before.

The weekend was strained. I had the urge to shout it from the rooftops, to tell his housemates and all we met of my condition, as I loved J and this should have been the happiest of times. Yet I respected and understood his request that this be kept between the two of us to avoid embarrassment in front of his mates.

At these times, I wish that mobile phones had been invented. It would have been comforting to know I could text him or my friend Kathy when I was feeling panicky on the train home to face a difficult week or while waiting for my appointment in the stark BPAS waiting room.

This was going to be one of those weeks you just want to get to the end of as quickly as possible or would rather you could avoid altogether.

There was nowhere I could run, physically or metaphorically. I had no choice but to square up to the fact that I needed to go through the process. The process began on the first floor of the intimidating Victorian red-brick British Pregnancy Advisory Service building in Navigation Street, Birmingham. I was exceedingly nervous. I sat in the waiting room beating myself up. I shouldn't be here, I thought. Indeed, I wouldn't be here if only I had been more sensible and realised that this could happen to me. If I hadn't lived assuming it wouldn't happen to me as my periods were few and far between. If we hadn't thrown caution to the wind, then this would never have happened, and I wouldn't be facing possibly the hardest decision of my life so far. It seemed an age before I was called into an interview room. The suited gentleman behind the desk took down my details; name, age, address, occupation, the usual. He raised his head and looked at me in a condescending manner when I admitted to being a second-year physiotherapy student. He intimated that someone of my educational standard shouldn't be in this situation. He asked how this could be and I mumbled some kind of inadequate reply to the effect that I had thought I was safe as my periods were so infrequent. This was deemed to be irresponsible, and it was, I suppose. He then outlined the way my appointment would be conducted. An internal examination by a doctor – male, of course – that would determine how far along I was and therefore the options I had. He explained that the law stated that an abortion (I'm not certain if the word termination was used at this point) was only permitted should the physical or mental health of the mother be considered to be at risk. Now I had an extra layer of fear. I may be considered not eligible if the doctor decided I didn't fit the criteria. It was all in his hands, I had no say, it seemed. He told me I would then be informed of the doctor's decision before leaving. I sat quietly, my stomach tight outwardly and churning inwardly.

A shroud of shame settled around my shoulders.

All self-esteem was sucked out of the room, leaving one frightened teenager looking down at her lap as her inquisitor continued to heap one negative emotion after another upon her. I walked back to the waiting room before being called for my examination.

It was a tiny room, just large enough for a couch and chair. I climbed up awkwardly and lay down on my back on the couch. I was trembling with fear. If only J was holding my hand. It was such a cold, harsh atmosphere. I tried to relax my legs as the male doctor requested that I bend them up and allowed them to flop open, but it wasn't easy. I turned my head to look at the magnolia painted wall, telling myself it would soon be over, recalling the time, not that long ago, when I had laid back and thought of England while locked in the bedroom of a university student. That was December. A sudden pang of realisation hit me. Could this be his child, not J's? As if that would *matter* in the grander scheme of things.

It was over. The doctor also explained the criteria and asked me about my living arrangements and any prior mental health issues. I told him I was at college training as a physio and that I wanted to complete my course. I dressed and returned to the waiting room to await my fate.

It was agreed that I met the criteria; how, I don't know! It looked as if there was a loophole somewhere that allowed them to sign my unborn child's death warrant. My doctor had previously requested I bring the paper confirming this eligibility to her surgery as soon as possible after being seen, so she could make the necessary arrangements. I took the two buses to get to the surgery that afternoon and once again awaited my turn around the carousel that was the busy surgery waiting room. There seemed nowhere to turn and no way to escape what now seemed to be inevitable. I was on the teenage unexpected pregnancy conveyor belt chugging through the system as if I was a piece of meat that needed trimming, just a number, an unfortunate occurrence that needed to be swept under the carpet and forgotten about. There was a cloak of silence around the whole process. The college principal wasn't aware as I'd been told to say I had a stomach bug and would be off sick for a few days, and my fellow students, apart from Kathy, weren't aware, although I always wondered if some of them had guessed what was happening.

I was thankful that Dr B called me in at the very start of surgery. No more waiting that day. She too explained the law of the land and what the letter from the clinic said and had meant. The doctor had written that I was, in his opinion, about ten weeks pregnant, so there was no time to lose. The cutoff date was twelve weeks, I think, for the simplest type of abortion. We had to move fast. While I sat in her surgery, she rang a clinic she knew nearby and made an appointment for me to attend the next week. That was it. All sorted. I still hadn't completely taken in what was happening as it was all going so fast with no time to reflect. Everyone was pushing me along as if on a plank in the pirate tales of my childhood, pushing me closer to the end of the board to the point of no return, regardless of my thoughts, my feelings, my faith and the fact that I felt this was against everything I believed was ethical and right. I had, in the last year, stated that I would never have an abortion, yet here I was heading towards the very action I despised. How could it be? How could I go through this thing that was abhorrent to me in others? How could I not? More imminently (and worryingly) how was I going to tell my parents that weekend?

CHAPTER 6

TIME TO PUT MY BIG GIRL PANTS ON

Still Aged 19: February 1979

Before I knew it, Friday arrived. I was on the coach, heading home from Northfield, to be met by my mother who, at that point, was doing the *Telegraph* crossword totally unaware of the turmoil in my life, as she patiently waited for me, sitting in her navy-blue Mini at the coach station. I tried to concentrate on the purple-covered physiology file open on my lap, as we had a test the following week on the filtration system of the kidney. Yet try as I might, the words just swam in front of my eyes, and I found myself reading the same paragraph over and over again without taking in a single word. The only filtration going on was that of the past fortnight's events that my brain was still struggling to digest. I found myself re-running each emotional blow interspersed by thoughts of how I was going to broach the subject with my mum and dad tomorrow afternoon.

I was extremely thankful of J's offer to join me and

face my parents as a united front, knowing that my father in particular would respect him for facing his responsibilities. We had arranged that he would come over mid-afternoon ostensibly to pick me up to go back to his parents' house for supper. Despite knowing my adoptive parents since I was six weeks old, I couldn't accurately read them and wasn't sure how they would respond. Would there be stony silence, or would there be shouting and accusation? One thing was certain: I would be thought of as a disgrace to the family. It wasn't something they would want their respectable middle-class friends and neighbours to get wind of. I'd never felt so scared and anxious of telling them anything in my life.

I caught sight of Mum's car as the coach swung round into the coach station. She was standing, her elbows leaning on the roof, in her trusty blue anorak, beige slacks and well-worn, zipped, fleecy, brown ankle boots. She raised her hand in a wave and smiled as she caught my eye. A warm glow swept through my body. I was a child in trouble just wanting her mum to hug her and tell her everything would be all right. For the next few hours, everything would be fine. I decided to enjoy the calm before the storm.

The journey home took around forty minutes on a good day and that day the traffic was light. She chatted easily about her week's events, the regular Scrabble Club meeting, the morning coffee at a friend's to cut her hair and the daily tasks of gardening, punctuated by a trip to the local village cafe each Friday for a lunch of homemade, delicious pie and vegetables from the local farm, followed by a slice of treacle tart and custard, her sweet of choice.

Despite the fact that my parents had moved house the day after I went to college, prompting many a remark that they were trying to get rid of me, I felt a strong sense of peace and happiness when I walked through the front porch and into the hallway. I was home. Home was mostly a safe and happy place to be. I was glad to have arrived and quickly unpacked my weekend bag as Mum busied around warming up the supper, usually something to – as she put it – warm up your cockles, maybe a lamb mince dish with mashed potatoes and fresh veg from her garden. I was hungry after the journey, not having eaten since my lunchtime meal in the hospital canteen. Meals were always eaten sitting around the family dining table and my task was to lay out the colourful placemats depicting countryside scenes and silver-plated cutlery inherited from my grandmother. Glasses of water were duly poured, and the meal dished up.

Dad usually had his head buried in the pages of a newspaper or was watching the news when I arrived home. I had popped my head round the lounge door to say hello when I first walked in, but knew it was best to leave him to read or listen to the TV until it was time to call him in for supper.

After eating, I offered to help with the washing up

and making the after-supper coffees and then enjoyed settling into an olive-green comfy armchair in front of the electric fire to sip my drink accompanied by a chocolate mint if I was lucky. This was the comfortable routine played out each time I came home. It was predictable. It was welcoming. And I felt very much at ease and at home.

Thankfully, the morning sickness had started to ease and was more a feeling of nausea. I didn't want my mum to guess that I was pregnant before we told her, that would have been far too scary to contemplate, so I acted as normally as possible, eating the same cereal, white rolls with honey and a cup of coffee for breakfast, going out for a walk mid-morning down the muddy lane that ran past the bungalow towards the common in the cold February air to get some exercise before lunch.

Everything was as normal, yet everything was far from normal. In just a few hours, it would all change and I feared the relaxed atmosphere would be ripped apart by our shameful secret being exposed. This wasn't how I had imagined it. I'd imagined the excitement of telling my parents they were to be grandparents for the first time and their delight at hearing the news. That was not to be. Being pregnant by accident while partway through my studies was not the kind of news they would want to hear. This kind of thing didn't happen to respectable girls, so what did that make me?

The mantelpiece clock ticked on – it seemed

so slowly – as I pretended to read the weekend supplement. Five past, ten past, twelve minutes past three. Each time I looked up, my stomach turned over a little and another knot of anxiety appeared until I was almost sick. Inside, my mind was in turmoil. I was frantically rehearsing how I would frame the words I needed to say, knowing there was no easy way to soften the blow, to lessen their disappointment in me or to reduce the impact.

At last, I saw him, the pale green of his dad's car appearing round the corner of the private road. I wondered if he was feeling as anxious as I was; I guess he probably was. I guess he was also most fearful of my dad's reaction, as he knew he had what was called "a bit of a short fuse".

J was liked by my parents. He was a kind grammar-school boy now studying civil engineering, who conversed easily about rugby with my dad and was happy to help Mum with her crossword if required. He was thought of as suitable boyfriend material for their only adopted daughter. Was that all about to change?

So here we were on a cold afternoon in February, all sitting in the lounge. Dad by the TV, J opposite the fire, and Mum and I on the settee facing Dad.

There was a bit of trivial conversation, you know the sort of thing, asking how J was and how his course was going, comments about the weather and asking after the health of his parents. Then there was a natural pause. It was me who spoke next. Looking to J for courage, with just a brief glance at my parents in turn, I said we had something to tell them. They were quiet, eyes fixed on me. Waiting. I wonder if they'd guessed or whether they thought we had decided to get engaged without asking for their consent. They must have noticed that I was nervous, but they allowed me to continue. How I didn't want to continue right then. How I wanted to wave a magic wand and change the whole sorry situation. How I needed all my strength to continue at this point. How nervous J must have been too.

There was no delaying the moment any longer.

"I'm pregnant," I said hurriedly, eyes flitting first to J and then to my mum, begging for compassion not condemnation, and then to my lap. I couldn't look over to my dad, I just couldn't. Mum was first to speak, in a measured way, cool but not angry, asking questions as to how many weeks I was and listening as the last two weeks spilled out in a torrent of emotion. I was aware that my six-foot-two-inch tall father had stood up. I could see he was struggling to contain his emotions. He walked behind J's chair and out of the lounge, out of the house. It wasn't to be the last time that I would be seen as a disappointment by him. It wasn't the last time that he would turn his back on me when I was in trouble, either.

Mum, however, was obviously very upset and not best pleased with either of us, but she did stay in the room, and we were able to have this very painful conversation with her. She listened in stony silence throughout and agreed to take me to the clinic and back on the date arranged by the doctor. I now understand how hard this was for her. Having tried for many years to conceive herself and feeling a failure for not being able to have her own child, she'd now found out her adopted daughter was pregnant with a child she hadn't planned or wanted. Life seemed to be laughing in her face.

I was never more relieved to leave the house than that day. Even though we were driving to J's house to tell his parents the news, I felt nervous but not as anxious as I had three quarters of an hour previously. We had time to talk it through as we drove. I thanked J for having the courage to turn up. I don't know how I would have done any of this without his support.

At his parents' home, I felt rather sheepish sitting on the beige settee, sitting on my hands to stop them shaking. The reaction this time was rather cool, no raised voices, just tangible disappointment. I had let everyone down. I had consequently taken a sharp fall in their estimation. I wished I could wave a magic wand and put everything back to how it was, but I couldn't. I had to see this thing through. No one had to say a word, as I felt ashamed enough without anything being added. I was already suffering for our carelessness and naivety. How could this be happening to us? This wasn't how I had imagined life to be.

The weekend and the support I felt with J by my side came to an end far too quickly. He went back to his studies, and I stayed home.

CHAPTER 7

UNEXPECTED KINDNESS

Still aged 19: February 1979

The dreaded clinic appointment was on Tuesday. Monday was the slowest day ever. I felt so conflicted. I wanted to change my mind many times that day, to speak up for my unborn child, but I was too scared to rock the boat. At no point had anyone suggested keeping the baby was an option to be seriously considered, quite the opposite. Only I had made a list of pros and cons of doing so.

The hardest thought was knowing I wouldn't be alive myself if my birth mother had made the choice I was making.

I hadn't thought of looking for my birth mother at this point in my life, but later I did find her. She empathised with my inner turmoil of this time, telling me she had struggled too and then found it so hard to give me up. There were other similarities in our circumstances, naivety and age being two. Looking back, I wish I had known her earlier. There was a hole in my life from not knowing my roots until I was in my early forties, which caused me to suffer from separation anxiety and to have a tendency to cling on to others emotionally out of a fear of losing them. This led to me getting into some seriously dangerous situations later in life.

Tuesday morning dawned. There was no more time. Today was the day it would end, or so I thought.

There was an uneasy silence in Mum's car as we drove to the Midlands. There wasn't anything left to say. My mouth was dry, my stomach uncomfortable and churning over. I spent the time looking out of the passenger window thinking of J and searching my mind for some reassuring happy memories to comfort myself. I wondered what he was feeling and thinking right then. Was he sad, distracted or relieved things would soon be over? Life without mobile phones could be hard. No text message to tell me he loved me and was thinking of me. No way of reaching across the miles in an instant. It was just me and Mum, and then it was just me, as Mum wasn't allowed to stay.

I can see the room, the white metal-framed bed I was in, and I can remember what the doctor told me a short while before I was taken to the anaesthetic room. They said that on examination they thought I may be too far along to have the procedure and, if that was the case, I would have to give birth. The fear and shock their words evoked caused me to scream throughout the procedure. I know this as I asked why my neck was so sore afterwards and was told they had to hold me down as I was screaming so much. This image still haunts me today. This really was me being pushed off the end of the pirate's plank into the deadly ocean below, having resisted as best as I could all the way along.

The redeeming memory of that day at the clinic was being able to help a young Spanish girl in the bed next to me. She was in a far worse predicament, having had to travel to the UK, as abortion was illegal in her country. She didn't speak English but understood a little and her eyes spoke the language of fear. Being a physio student, I demonstrated deep breathing and told her to do this as soon as she woke up to get rid of the anesthetic. I held her hand until it was my turn to go down to the anaesthetist's room. It was the language of human kindness. When I returned, she somehow was already back beside me. It was me gasping for air and she who reached out to hold my hand and said "breathe" in a gentle Spanish accent. My mother returned to collect me and take me home, bringing with her a jar of honey, my preferred toast topping.

Throughout my life, kindness given has often returned to me at the darkest of moments.

CHAPTER 8

ALL CHANGE!

Age 20-21: 1979-1980: College Year 2-3

Physically I healed quickly with no health concerns. Lying has always been difficult for me, the truth is usually plastered all over my face, but it was of paramount importance, I was told, that I returned to college saying I had been sent home with a stomach upset, as this is what the college doctor had told the principal. I wonder sometimes if she or the other staff guessed the truth, but I held up my end of the bargain and no one questioned my story.

It was life as usual, my "dirty little secret" had been swept under the carpet never to be spoken of again. My family could once again hold their heads up high, having successfully dodged an extremely awkward social faux pas. I played my part well to begin with but began to notice I had started to have sudden unexpected outbursts of anger at times, resulting on one occasion in a used pudding bowl being hurled across the kitchen of J's shared high-rise flat one afternoon, crashing on the stone floor and breaking into a thousand pieces of white china spattered with yellow custard.

College became less enjoyable, and I began to struggle with the work. I didn't fit in somehow, I felt an outcast from the girls I was sharing a flat with and I thought they disliked me. Life wasn't at all fun except at the weekends, which was the only thing keeping me going at that time.

Then one day, I decided enough was enough, I didn't want to be at college any more, I had to get out. So I did. One late evening, on a whim, I summoned the courage to run away. I found myself at Birmingham New Street late at night waiting for a train to Sheffield. It was almost empty, and I felt nervous being in a carriage on my own, having heard horror stories of what had happened to women travelling alone by train late at night. I hadn't contacted J before I left as I knew he would have tried to talk me out of it. I just imagined arriving unannounced and being welcomed in and listened to over a cup of hot chocolate and a hug.

What I hadn't imagined was a totally empty house with all the lights blazing past midnight. Where were they all? What was going on? I decided to make myself a cup of tea and wait for someone to come back. It was a long wait before Phil, J's best friend, staggered in through the front door, slightly the worse for wear, before stopping dead in his tracks as he saw me in the living area. I gathered from him that it was freshers' week and everyone was down at the students' union building. He asked me why I was there and quickly disappeared to warn J of my presence, I assumed.

I wondered what reaction I would get from him. He would have had a few pints himself and should have been in a genial mood. I was lucky that J rarely got angry with anyone and never after a few beers!

I enjoyed a much-needed cup of tea and watched the TV for what seemed an age before I heard them chatting in urgent and rather loud tones as they drew closer to the door.

"Hi!" I exclaimed in a rather lame voice as J appeared round the door, closely followed by Phil. Though not outwardly upset with me, I sensed I had pooped on his party, turning up unannounced as I had.

I got the impression that he'd rather I hadn't known about the exploits of freshers' week, but that was the least of my worries. I told him I was sorry to just arrive, but that I couldn't cope at college any more and didn't know where else to run. He appeared to have taken in the situation and cracked open a can of beer before sitting beside me to listen to my woes.

Phil, I noticed, smiled and made his excuses; no doubt hotfooting it back down to the union building with the latest information to tell the rest of J's friends.

Looking back, though never diagnosed, I think I was suffering from post-traumatic stress disorder. I had started bursting into tears for no apparent reason and found college life unbearable. The coursework and practical assignments suddenly seemed much harder to get my head around and my flatmates were distant and cold towards me, or so it seemed. I couldn't see a clear path in front of me. Everything looked bleak.

The only place I wanted to be was with J, wherever that may be. Day or night, weekday or weekend, I wanted to be by his side. His presence made me feel safe and complete. He didn't get angry with me, even when I had an anger outburst. He listened and he seemed to understand me. If I could have moved up to Sheffield that very week and transferred onto the physio course up there I would have done so.

However, the fact that this didn't happen probably saved our relationship. If I had been there 24/7 it may have been too much for J to deal with. He needed his own space to socialise with his housemates and the other poly students in his year. He needed other conversations with nights on the piss and afternoons playing rugby to have a chance to manage his own emotions around recent events.

That night, however, he was everything I needed him to be. A confidant, a boyfriend, a guy who loved me deeply and shared my experience and my pain.

Having got my deepest thoughts and feelings off my chest and had a good cry and a reassuring hug, I managed to sleep.

We had agreed to work out a solution the next morning when we weren't as emotional and could think more clearly. After a good breakfast, we sat down to formulate a plan. The first thing was to let someone know that I was safe, that no one had abducted – or worse, killed me – on the streets of Birmingham the night before, that I wasn't lying in a ditch somewhere dead or in need of medical attention. We walked to the phone box a few minutes away from the student areas. I waited for the time on his watch to say 10.10am, then, full of fear, I called the phone number for the college common room that served tea and coffee from 10am each day. I was hoping I could ask to speak to my best friend Kathy to let her know I was safe. I did get to talk to her but was surprised to find out she had been told to ask me for the phone box telephone number so the principal could ring me back and speak to me.

I obediently did as asked, then put the receiver down, relaying the short conversation to J. I waited for the tinny ring of the public phone. It rang a few minutes later. The principal was speaking. She spoke quietly and calmly in her soft German accent, immediately reassuring me that I wasn't in trouble and asking me to tell her why I had run away. That helped me to feel heard. I still couldn't tell her the full story but emphasised my unhappiness in my shared house and recent difficulty with the coursework. She kept a steady, gentle tone throughout and asked me to return on the Birmingham train that afternoon and go straight to college for a private meeting with her. That way I wouldn't have to explain myself to any of my year group on the way as they'd all be at their hospital placements.

It gave me a few hours to talk things through with J and decide what I was going to request in this upcoming meeting.

I really needed to move out of that accommodation somehow, but I couldn't see where else I could go. We did talk through the options of me quitting my course to transfer up to Sheffield, but he suggested that was a bit radical and that there may be an easier solution. I wasn't sure what my immediate future held; I just knew something had to change.

The train journey was uneventful and there was even a number 63 bus waiting to whisk me down the Bristol Road. That's a bit of artistic licence, as the 61, 62 and 63 buses were the snails of the public transport system in that part of the city and rarely got above 40mph, at a guess.

I think J was relieved I had gone back to college. He had his own studies to attend and would have already had to come up with a plausible excuse as to why he'd been absent at morning lectures.

Eventually, my bus crawled up the final rise to the hospital where my college was based. I can see it now, forty-two years on, as clearly as if it were yesterday!

I walked past the tiny hydrotherapy building and round the driveway past the orthopaedic wards to the School of Physiotherapy at the far end of the site, opposite a bank of mature trees. My heart by this time was beating a little fast. I was experiencing a mix of anxiety, relief, familiarity at being "home" and shame to name a few. Again, if only there were mobile phones in those days. How much better I would have felt if I could have enlisted virtual support from J and my friend Kathy. I knew Kathy would be praying, as she was a keen Christian, which gave me some comfort, and I shot up a few arrow prayers of the "Please help me!" kind myself as I neared the front entrance.

Feeling awkward on entering the building, I didn't have to wait for more than a couple of seconds before I heard the secretary phoning to let the principal know I had arrived. She was in her office as her door opened and I saw her walking towards me in her characteristic tweed suit and slight limp. She smiled and ushered me into her domain and to the waiting chair across the desk from hers.

I don't know how many times she had conducted such a conversation, if I was the first to abscond or the twenty-first, but she handled things with quiet authority, giving me the respect I so needed by listening carefully as the sorry story came tumbling out. I tried to maintain my composure, but the tears seeped out in ones and twos before the floodgates broke and my face turned red with emotion and embarrassment.

As I mentioned before, I couldn't see a way round my predicament, except by leaving to go back home or move to Sheffield. What I hadn't considered was the option she suggested.

Apparently, in particular circumstances, students were allowed to move back into the nurses' home,

Elizabeth Cadbury House, where I'd spent my first year on the first floor.

The top-floor rooms were a little better than the first-year student rooms, having a small basin in them, and as there were only a handful of girls living there, the kitchen, laundry room, toilet block and bathroom were less crowded.

The block was centrally heated with plenty of hot running water, which now seemed a complete luxury compared to the Victorian ice block I had been sharing for the past six months. The girls I'd been sharing with would feel happier too with more space and no more awkwardness around me. It was a no-brainer, as my younger friends would say.

My main concern was how to tell my parents. I felt I had failed by not thriving in my challenging living conditions, which Mum had thought were palatial compared to her boarding school accommodation. I had let them down again.

Once more, I was rescued. Maybe there was a God after all! I didn't have to make that phone call. They hadn't been informed of my sudden departure from college, as I had called in to say I was safe, and it was agreed that they would accept the information better if the principal phoned to explain that there had been an altercation with my housemates, which would be resolved by me moving back into the first-year student housing block on the college site.

I loved my new room. It was less than five minutes'

walk from the college and the hospital canteen. It was warm on the coldest winter day. I could have a hot bath whenever I chose, and the food didn't get stolen out of the shared fridge. What more could I have asked for?

I certainly started to feel more myself after a few weeks and was looked up to by the first years who didn't know my situation but who I chatted to in the TV lounge. They were pleased to be able to ask about what was coming up for them in the first-year practical exam and I was a willing model for them to trace out the course of the radial nerve or the anterior saphenous vein.

I was accepted, I was liked and, in their eyes, I was more than enough.

I became a bit of an agony aunt too, always happy to lend a listening ear to a first year whose heart had been broken or who was struggling with home sickness.

I now realise this was the first time of many in my life that I would use my own experience to gain insight and be able to listen and empathise with others.

[As an aside: this is the rationale behind me writing to you here. To make sense of my journey and walk alongside you, as you make sense of yours; assuring you of your innate enough-ness, no matter what's been hurled at you physically or metaphorically!]

Life improved dramatically from that moment. Year two ended and the summer holidays were glorious, peppered with reunions of school friends and outings to the seaside and local beauty spots for picnics and walks with J and with Mum, seeing my grandparents and generally smiling at this new lease of life.

CHAPTER 9

NEW HORIZONS AHEAD

Age 20-21: College final year: Sept 1979-Summer 1980

I am thankful that I didn't quit, didn't give up on my dream of being a physiotherapist, didn't transfer up to Sheffield.

My joie de vivre had returned. I looked forward to college and my hospital placements each day and I began to see the light at the end of the dark tunnel I had been travelling down since February.

I still had flashbacks of that day I gave up on my unborn child, with pangs of guilt, sadness and shame. I still found these were triggered by soap opera storylines, seeing new mums in the park at weekends, special days like Mother's Day and Father's Day and walking into church, which brought my guilt quickly to the surface.

As a practising – and I stress practising, not perfect – Christian, it was particularly hard to justify my actions to myself or to anyone else. How could I have taken a course of action that was so opposite to my belief in the sanctity of life?

This was the first of several situations where I realised that faith wasn't as black and white as I had first imagined, where other factors came into play to cause me to behave in a way I would have previously denounced and judged others for. It was an important lesson to learn and helped me to become more understanding and tolerant of others.

Overall, 1980 was a happy and successful year. We were all busy completing the assignments and practical assessments essential to qualify in the summer. I recall failing my passive movement skills twice and just getting it signed off a day or so before the deadline.

I enjoyed researching my project and was fortunate to have a gentleman with this very condition, osteoarthritis of the hip, for my final practical exam in June, where I completed a verbal and practical assessment and answered the examiner's questions regarding my findings and proposed treatment plan.

It was over! I walked out of the cubicle with a relieved smile on my face and hoped I had done enough to pass.

A few months beforehand, I was engaged to J, who even asked for my dad's blessing. A very different vibe to a year earlier. I think he had won them over by his willingness to take responsibility for his part in the pregnancy and to stick by me afterwards. We had a celebration meal at home, with mum helping me to cook a steak and mushroom pie, which was much loved by everyone.

I thought the dark days immediately after the termination were behind me, but I was to realise several years later on that they hadn't been completely buried.

Everyone loves an awards ceremony, and I was so proud to invite J and my parents to witness me being presented with my badge that I would wear every day on my tunic lapel. We didn't know at this point who had passed or failed but we had all completed the course, which qualified us to receive this token together with a single red rose. I felt special, and I seemed to have finally met my parents' expectations of me.

This was confirmed with the news a few weeks later that I had passed with flying colours. I was a newly qualified chartered physiotherapist and it felt amazing!

I had already secured a job placement that specialised in stroke rehabilitation at a hospital on the outskirts of Sheffield where J was in his final year to qualify as a civil engineer. We would finally be able to live together, me working and earning a small wage while he completed his course.

Finding accommodation proved a little more troublesome, but a week before I was due to start, we heard our application for a housing association flat had been accepted. Phew! That was a bit close!

This was in a new-build block of flats close to City Hall and opposite the fire station. Our flat was on the inside of a quadrangle, so we didn't hear the weekly fire practice as loudly as our neighbours on the street side, but it was reassuring to know they were just a stone's throw away should there be an emergency. It turned out that the fire alarm system was a bit trigger happy and had a habit of sounding at two o'clock in the morning. This became such a regular feature of life there that it became dangerous, as no one would take any notice of it. Having been shown a particularly gruesome film of a real fire in an Australian hospital as part of my induction, I was always careful to check it was just a false alarm, and luckily it always was.

It felt strange to be a qualified member of staff. My confidence was rather shaky to start with and I would always ask my superior before starting a treatment plan. She was kind yet firm in her response, reassuring me that my work was of a good standard, and we agreed on a monthly check in to ask questions and for her to give me feedback.

We were part of a small staff team covering geriatrics (now known as elderly care), rheumatology, stroke rehabilitation inpatient and outpatient day centre and maternity unit.

Strangely, I most enjoyed working on the maternity wards where I taught pre- and post-natal classes, checked the caesarean section new mums, gave general advice on circulation, breathing after the anaesthetic and teaching pelvic floor exercises to those who'd recently given birth naturally. There was a friendly atmosphere on this unit, and I got on well with all the staff, it was a lovely way to end each day.

Surprisingly, I didn't feel triggered by this work. In fact, if I could have stayed there all day, I would have been more than happy. This could have been due to difficulties fitting in with the other therapy staff. I'm not sure why, but I just didn't seem to fit, no matter how hard I tried.

It wasn't long before J's course was completed, and his parents came up to see him in all his regalia for his graduation ceremony. Getting work, however, was much harder for him, as the slump in the early 1980s meant hundreds of applicants chasing any and every job. I tried to support him where I could, spending many an hour typing out job enquiry letters only for him to get another rejection letter or not hear anything back at all. After the one-hundredth knock-back, J started to look further afield. Any job was better than none and would give him a reference to be able to use. He worked on a delivery van for a while, I remember, though this turned out to cause grief with his social security payments, before we decided to move further south, as this would give him a better chance of getting a job and I could start afresh somewhere where I hopefully would feel happier.

In the physio world, jobs are advertised in the monthly *Physiotherapy* journal. I applied for jobs in Truro, Oxford and Coventry. It was a harsh, snowy winter and I got interviews for all three of these. As it turned out, I could only physically get to one of them. Many trains were cancelled due to snow drifts. I managed to get halfway to Truro, having to get off at Exeter and retrace my steps to Gloucester.

The Oxford interview was a no-go from the start due to the atrocious weather conditions, but I finally made it to Coventry. It was the city centre hospital, called the Coventry & Warwickshire Hospital, specialising in orthopaedics with a busy outpatient department and intensive care unit. I was offered the job on the spot and accepted.

We were going to be heading back south!

CHAPTER 10

HEADING SOUTH AGAIN

Age 22-25: 1982-1985

My start date was almost immediate, giving us little chance to find a rental property, so I was offered a room in the nurses' home on the site of Walsgrave Hospital on the outskirts of the city.

I could use the staff canteen and there was a regular bus service into Coventry Central Bus Station, making my first few weeks easier than I had expected. I was particularly thankful for the warmth of the central heating as the cold snap continued for a while after I started. J visited me every couple of weeks, and I scoured the rental housing column of the local paper and asked for suggestions from my fellow physios for a suitable place to move into.

As it turned out, I happened to see a small card pinned to the notice board in the entrance hall of my temporary accommodation on my way out to catch the bus one morning:

Flat for rent
(Gresley Road)
2 bedrooms
First floor
Free parking
£220 pm

It also had a contact name and number.

My heart missed a beat. Checking no one was watching, I unpinned the card, not wanting anyone else to jump in before me. I tucked it into the bank note section of my red purse and almost skipped to the bus stop. There was a clear blue sky and a cool wind, a perfect crisp spring day. I couldn't wait to ask my new friend Shirley where Gresley Road was, whether it was in an okay part of town and buy a local map to locate it. It turned out not to be the most salubrious of areas, but it was at the end of a quiet cul-de-sac with a green space and stream on one side and a mobile home park at the top of the road. The flats were modern, a small complex on three sides of a square, just three storeys high. Beryl, the blonde-haired physio receptionist, kindly let me use the phone to call the owner, a young guy named Rob. I arranged for J to collect me from outside the nurses' home a couple of evenings later to view it.

As soon as I walked up the stairway and through the dark mauve front door, I felt at home. The flat was warm and cosy, decorated in a modern if bright style and spacious. The sky-blue kitchen looked out over a grassy area lined with conifers behind the flats with the stream to the left. The most exciting room, decoratively speaking, was the main bedroom, which sported bright red floorboards. I could see those would need covering with an off-cut of carpet as soon as possible! We looked at each other, smiled, nodded and agreed to take it, paying two months' rent up front. Rob arranged to call round every month for the rent cheque and to ensure everything was well from his point of view and from ours.

I was excited to move in, to be back living with J again, this time on a more permanent basis, and to feel more settled.

Moving day was hilarious. J's friend Chris hired a retired red post office van, an old rickety thing with side sliding doors that didn't want to stay shut. We packed all our possessions into the back of the van, only just able to close the doors, and set off, three of us across the ripped front seat, on the long, bumpy journey from Sheffield to Coventry. It reminded me of the *Pink Panther* car chase scene, bouncing around, and I can still hear the music now. We swayed and bumped our way down the road, almost hitting our heads on the roof each time we hit a rut, all the time praying the side and back doors wouldn't suddenly spring open and scatter all of our life possessions across the carriageway. Luckily, we made it in one piece, picking up my bits and bobs, before Chris returned said van from whence it came. I never *did* know who he'd borrowed it from or how much it had cost him, but I believe it was under £50. Cheap and cheerful was our motto and it certainly was the source of many a happy memory.

The next chapter had begun. Our challenge now was to find J a job.

At St Bernard's Road, Sutton Coldfield with Timmy our
stray "Heinz variety" breed dog who followed Mum home
one day and stayed until he was sixteen years old

Enjoying the flowers at my grandpa's house

My adopted
mum who
loved the sun

Dad at
Woolacombe
beach on
our annual
Whitsun
week
holiday

My school, Stroud Girls High, the senior block.
I attended school here from 1970 – 1977

Mum
sitting on
the back
doorstep
with Lara
and Bella,
her best
friend's
dogs

Aged 18 showing off my tan in the sea at Bournemouth

My first
year room
in Liz
Cad with
the large
teddy J
gave me
and my
handmade
patchwork
cushion

Dad and
I walking
on the
common
in the
college
Christmas
break,
1977

One of my favourite photos of my adopted mum
taken in her heyday

CHAPTER 11

BIG STEPS FORWARD

Age 22-24: 1982-1984: Coventry

The change of location seemed to trigger a change in luck, as J quickly found a position with an earthwork business as a junior engineer in nearby Wellingborough. This came with a spacious Peugeot estate car, which made a huge difference to us. Feeling more settled, I began to grow in my desire to get my driving licence under my belt before embarking on starting a family. One of my physio colleagues suggested the instructor she had just passed with, so I bit the bullet, made the phone call and booked an initial package of ten lessons starting the following week. Shortly afterwards, the nerves kicked in.

I was to meet her on Wednesday, straight after work, at the start of the rush hour, outside the gates of the hospital in the heart of the city. Was I mad? It was 5pm and I was on my first driving lesson. You can guess how my stomach was churning. Looking back, I can imagine how frustrating it must have been for the drivers who encountered me that afternoon. I am chastened these days when I'm tempted to think, "Bl***y learner driver!" when crawling along at 30mph on the dual carriageway out of my local market town. I was there once!

My driving instructor was such a patient lady, yet the years of being an instructor had taken its toll. I didn't quite take in the extent of the anxiety she faced on a daily basis at the time, but on reflection I recall being requested to pull over most weeks during my drive for her to pick up her tranquillisers. Was I really that bad?

I was a keen learner and picked things up quickly, the only problem being reversing round a corner. Despite the strategically placed stickers on the rear and side windows, I struggled to get my head round which way to turn the wheel and at what point. My test day turned out to be a dry, sunny one in the May half term holiday week, at lunchtime, so the roads were full of business traffic and parents transporting their children to various leisure activities. It was chaotic.

All went well until the examiner told me to make a right turn at an upcoming T-junction. We were in a tree-lined residential area on this bright sunny day. I indicated left by mistake for a brief moment, but quickly apologised and corrected my mistake. As I approached the junction, I looked right, left and right again as I had been taught, before pulling out. As I did so, I glanced left and couldn't believe what my eyes were telling me. I responded by planting "both feet down", as my mum described an emergency stop, and came to a sudden stop without stalling or swerving. The instructor was as shocked as I was, bracing himself while looking left to see what had caused me to act in this way. There was a dark brown car driving out of the shadow of a tree. He hadn't seen it either! Quickly regaining his composure, but visibly surprised and shocked by the event, he directed me to continue to a safe place to pull in.

That was it, I thought. It was over, I had failed. I prepared for the calm delivery of this verdict, due to my lack of observation.

The words that came out of his mouth were totally unexpected. He praised my quick reactions saying that as he had missed the car himself my test wasn't over. Taking a deep breath, I pulled off and continued on the designated route. I still had to perform a test emergency stop when he sharply tapped his clipboard on the dashboard, which I executed perfectly and even my reverse round a corner was reasonable. After answering the *Highway Code* questions correctly, having brought the vehicle to a controlled halt next to the kerb, I was quietly informed that I had passed! I was delighted.

Well, how *could* he fail someone who had saved his life by stopping for a car he had failed to see himself?

That night, I bought a copy of the local paper and eagerly turned to the second-hand car pages at the back, as my bus turned out of the bus station heading towards Walsgrave. There's something about poring over a freshly printed paper, the smell of the ink and paper in your nostrils. I had a sense of excitement at what I might find hidden in the long list of vehicles for sale.

I wanted a small, economical car, easy to drive, giving me the opportunity to get about when J was at work.

It was only a matter of weeks after getting myself on the road that I discovered I was pregnant.

This time it was planned.

This time it was good news.

This time I was excited.

This time it wasn't a secret with stigma and shame attached to it.

This time my parents were pleased and happy to share the news with the rest of their family and friends.

This time it was going to be *so* different!

In my excitement to replay and relive these memories, I've realised I've totally skipped past the fact that J and I got married one bright, crisp spring day in April 1982, just a couple of months after moving into the flat.

The day was well planned by my adopted mum, who was renowned for her organisational skills. There were tick lists for everything, which were methodically worked through. She had a cunning way of appearing to listen to my thoughts on matters yet implementing her own decisions in whatever area of wedding planning we were talking about. The only parts I really felt reflected *my* thoughts, were the choice of venue and the date, which was the 10th of April, Easter Saturday that year, although even that was in doubt for a while and subject to us agreeing to use the traditional church flower arrangements for the Easter season, including traditional white lilies. My colour scheme fitted in perfectly with this; yellow, cream and white, which was reflected in the small triangular bouquets of freesias and lily of the valley, and white carnation buttonholes. The ceremony was held in the pretty village church where I attended Sunday school with my school friends and later attended confirmation classes. We decided on the well-known "Love is" passage from 1 Corinthians 13 for the reading and the older version of the vows, which included to love and obey.

The budget for my big day was decided by my chartered accountant father who told me we could keep anything that was left over, which sounded far more generous than it actually was.

I was shepherded through the process in a seamless manner. The bridesmaid was one of my godmother's daughters, Hilary, who I rarely saw. The reception venue was also Mum's choice and the menu definitely her domain as an expert in catering and home economics. Even the present list written by J and I was manipulated.

My greatest disappointment was the long-awaited

trip to look for a dress. I had anticipated this for two years, since our engagement, poring over bridal magazines and cutting out pictures of dresses I liked. I had great expectations of a beautiful expansive white creation from one of the prestigious bridal shops of the moment, Pronuptia. These gowns were near the top of the price range but fulfilled my longing to be transformed into the princess of my dreams for this long-awaited special day, my wedding day. It didn't turn out like that at all, ending up in the purchase of a reduced gown that wasn't at all what I'd set my heart on. I liked the dress we bought, and I think it suited me, it just wasn't what I had dreamt of!

The day itself went to plan, as I'm sure you had expected to read. My dad helped me into the white Ford Granada (not the Merc I had fantasised) and then proceeded to sit in the front talking to the driver about golf, even on this, his only child's wedding day!

I felt rejected, strangely abandoned, as if I were a chattel being dressed up and delivered to the church. We did the obligatory turn round the village as the groom hadn't arrived when we drew up but, other than that, it all went swimmingly. I spotted my college friend, Kathy, who would have been *my* choice of bridesmaid, as I walked down the aisle to the wedding music featured in *The Sound of Music* (not our choice) and I didn't fluff my words. We processed out to a triumphant piece I really did love, Bach's "Toccatta and Fugue in D Minor".

There being a cold wind, all the guests had decided to leave the church straight after the photos and had arrived at the reception ahead of us, so sadly there was no welcoming line as I had imagined, as they were already inside chatting in the bar. My uncle was master of ceremonies, and I found time just disappeared, only managing to talk to a few guests before being summoned to take my seat for the two course meal (not the buffet I had favoured). The speeches were funny without being offensive (phew!) and the whole event was over far too fast. Before I knew it, we were waving goodbye to our friends and family in a hired postbox-red Ford Escort to an unknown – to me, that is – destination. It turned out to be a four-star hotel on the cliffs of Lynmouth, Devon. Nine days later, I celebrated my twenty-third birthday by playing crazy golf and tucking into a plate of my favourite chateaubriand washed down with a glass of Chianti. Life was good.

CHAPTER 12

ONWARDS AND UPWARDS

Age 24-27: 1983-1985: Coventry and Swindon

Christmas was just around the corner; it was the time for preparations and celebrations. I treated myself to a luxurious cashmere jumper for the physio department Christmas dinner in early December, held at a much-recommended eatery in Kenilworth, to which partners were invited.

We enjoyed some time with family over the festive period and had just settled back into our work routines when I found myself pregnant.

This time was certain to be very different.

I was right.

Different, nauseous, strange, unexpected yet expected, amazing, weird, totally not what the books described, exciting, scary, the list of adjectives encompassed a whole spectrum of emotion!

Yes, I was officially pregnant, in the way it was supposed to be, according to the culture of the eighties:

☑ Married.
☑ Having worked so having a job to return to.
☑ Not too young.
☑ Not too old.

Despite meeting all the above criteria, I was still nervous about telling my parents, Mum in particular. It was still a taboo subject in our house since the abortion.

Yet, I thought, surely she would be happy this time and enjoy sharing the news of shortly becoming a grandmother with the neighbours? Wouldn't she? My heart was beating a little faster in my chest as I dialled the number and waited for her to answer the landline. After a few rings, her characteristic voice announced the exchange name and number and paused for a response.

"Hi, Mum," I said brightly. "We've got some exciting news for you," I quickly added. "You're going to be a granny."

Silence.

I glanced over to J sitting next to me with a nervous smile, while my fingers twisted the brown, coiled phone wire. How would she respond?

"Am I? That's lovely news, love."

Relief flooded over my face. Everything was going to be all right.

* * * * *

I was the first in the department to fall pregnant and everyone was excited for me. The morning sickness, however, was tricky to navigate, especially as I travelled the twenty minutes to work by bus. I used to dread the waves of nausea that swept over me, but somehow managed to get to the hospital before rushing to the ladies in the changing rooms to throw up. I'm pleased to say this phase was short lived, passing within a few weeks, and I started to feel more myself again. As I mentioned earlier, I had tussled with my weight since my teens, but finally I had no reason to beat myself up about my size and I celebrated the fact by eating for a football team rather than for two! It wasn't long before I was popping the buttons off my blue uniform trouser waistband and needing to wear A-line maternity tunic tops.

At about the six-month point in my pregnancy, we went on holiday to a small guest house in North Devon on the winding cliff road from Woolacombe to Morte Ho! Woolacombe had seen both of us growing up as children and remained a favoured summer break destination. The guest house was opposite a narrow path leading to a set of steep steps down to a beautiful sandy beach, which was just perfect. There were rock pools to fish in and the area was safe for swimming. I've always enjoyed taking a dip in the sea, despite the icy cold water making me squeal as it splashed up onto my tummy. I would stride purposefully through the smaller waves before taking the plunge just as a big wave was about to crash into my chest. That year, more than ever, I felt confident in my swimsuit, there being no reason to feel ashamed of my ballooning stomach. I felt very happy, even laughing as a powerful wave flipped me over onto my back, leaving me thrashing around like a beached whale in an attempt to get back onto my feet.

The sun shone. The days were long, lazy and filled with fun. The food was good, the company pleasant and the room small but comfortable. I was in love with my husband, the father of my unborn child and everything in my world was wonderful, just how I had imagined it, how it should be, in my way of thinking.

Hold that thought.

Mull over that memory. That doorway to happiness.

As I've grown older, I've learnt how important it is to savour these happy-go-lucky times as they happen, drinking in the moment, basking in them and enjoying the emotions they evoke when reminiscing.

I knew nothing at the time of what would befall us, befall me, as time progressed; all I could see was sunshine, sea and smiles, and in hindsight I am so grateful.

The summer of '84 was hot. After leaving work to start my maternity leave, I spent my days sitting in the garden at the back of the flats, walking to the local corner shop for a magazine, milk or chocolate and walking beside the stream that ran at the side of the property. It wasn't quite as idyllic as you may imagine, having more than its fair share of plastic bottles, beer cans, toilet tissue and shopping trolleys along its length. I've never understood why people feel the need to dispose of their rubbish this way, but it's been an ongoing and seemingly unsolvable problem throughout my lifetime to date.

It was 1984 and Los Angeles was hosting the Summer Olympic Games. The UK running interest that year was Sebastian Coe – or Seb, as he was known. Being home, having started my maternity leave in July, I took more of an interest in the games than usual and was excited to see Seb win his heats, getting through to the final of the men's 1500 metres. This final was held in the middle of the night in British time, so we were in bed. I was feeling uncomfortably large by this point, which meant sleep was sporadic. I crept out of the bedroom in my dressing gown to watch the race with the volume turned low so as not to wake J. It was a tense race with another Brit, Steve Cram, on his shoulder in the final straight. I sat on the edge of the sofa as Seb held him off to achieve his second Olympic gold medal at this distance in record time. I watched as he did a lap of honour, waving a Union Jack from one of the spectators. I had witnessed a moment in history. I turned the TV off and waddled back into the bedroom to the window, resting my forearms on the windowsill and looking out at the night sky. I so wanted to wake J and tell him Seb had defended the gold, but I knew he had to get up early for work the next day, so I couldn't, it wouldn't be fair.

The weeks seemed to drag by as I approached the nine-month mark and my gynaecologist fretted over the baby's size, requesting an X-ray, yes, an X-ray to check whether I would need a caesarean section. I couldn't believe it when the radiologist asked me to lie on my stomach. I questioned it, but yes, this was the position needed to get the images for the gynaecologist. Can you imagine the difficulty I had climbing onto the bed on all fours and then trying to lie on my bump? It was so uncomfortable. Thankfully she got good images on her first attempt and the measurements showed it would be a close call. I was to start my labour naturally, it was decided, but they were aware I may need an emergency caesarean section if the baby got stuck in the birth canal. Because of this possibility, I was deemed eligible for an epidural. That part I was relieved to hear, as it meant my pain relief would be well controlled, which being a first-time mum (though officially this was my second child) was what I was most anxious about.

The heatwave continued with temperatures in the eighties. I struggled to keep cool, despite drinking copious amounts of water and enjoying ice lollies throughout the day. The first floor flat seemed like a sauna with little breeze, despite having all the windows open. My initial due date was the 12th of August but I was well past that with no sign of even any Braxton Hicks practice contractions, let alone the real thing. I tried all manner of things to gee the process up. I ate hot curry, I jumped up and down, I tried to run up and down the stairs, all to no avail. As I was getting absolutely nowhere, it was decided that I should go into Walsgrave Hospital to be induced and give birth. I packed my bag and J took me in just before the August bank holiday weekend. It was just my luck that seemingly every pregnant lady in Coventry decided to go into labour over that weekend! I was told they had no beds in the labour ward due to a sudden influx of patients and that I wouldn't be induced until the ward quietened down. It was the Monday of the bank holiday weekend before it was finally my turn. The midwife gave me a pessary to start my contractions but without any success.

The next morning, having had a bath and shaved the required area, I had my waters broken to induce my labour. This resulted in the start of labour pains. I was surprised at the pain I felt. Contractions didn't feel at all like I had expected. I reminded the midwife that I was due to have an epidural, which was duly administered by the anaesthetist. The pain began to ease and so began The Long Wait.

There I lay, with J sitting on my right-hand side, being monitored for signs of contractions and levels of epidural. We talked about everything we could think of, including the holiday in Devon earlier in the year. When things became very uncomfortable and we had run out of conversation, I asked J to talk about his parents' dog, Robbie-dog. He was always getting into mischief, and I was able to distract my thoughts a bit by listening to his escapades that made me laugh. After almost seven hours, I was ready to move to the labour room. The time was here. The end of the road. The beginning of motherhood for me.

It wasn't quite so simple, though. The epidural meant I couldn't move my legs and they were hoisted up into stirrups, leaving me in a very ungainly position. The midwife needed to prompt me when to push to coincide with the contractions she was watching on her monitor. I had a bit of sensation but wasn't certain when they started or ended. I pushed as best as I could. They encouraged me, J held my hand, and I grabbed his hair at one point, I think! I was desperate to get this thing over with, to see my baby, but it wasn't ending. There was talk of forceps and caesarian sections, but finally I heard what I was waiting to hear: "The head is out. Pant, pant." I panted. I was exhausted. It was 7.30pm when Lucy Anne was born, a healthy baby girl weighing in at just over 8lb. She cried. They wrapped her up in a cellular blanket with just her head poking out and I held her. It was photo time!

Everything was going to be just fine.

I was ready for that cup of tea back on the postnatal ward. J stayed a while until the end of visiting time, and I felt very alone when he went. I was propped up in the bed and still couldn't move my legs properly. I became aware of a growing pain in my lower abdomen as if needing the toilet, but I couldn't pass water on the bedpan. The pain continued to increase, but the nurses didn't seem to be concerned. Eventually, they looked at me and decided I needed a catheter; such relief to be able to empty my bladder at last.

As I was feeling dizzy and unable to stand from the residual effects of the epidural, Lucy Anne was taken to the nursery and cared for overnight. I had started to talk to a lady in the opposite bed to me, who had given birth to a little girl, Hayley, just before me. I felt calmer and was finally able to drift off to sleep for a couple of hours.

I was a new mum!

CHAPTER 13

"WHY DIDN'T ANYONE WARN ME!?"

Age 25-26: 1984-1985

My first day of motherhood felt bewildering and scary. I was extremely tired, very sore everywhere down below and felt faint each time I stood up. It wasn't how I had imagined it or had seen it in films. I was told to feed my baby but had no idea how to do it. On requesting some assistance to breastfeed her, I was told to just get on with it, which made me feel tearful and inadequate when she didn't latch on or suck effectively. It wasn't a good start.

Mealtimes were held in a communal area a little walk from my bed. It was so painful to walk down the ward and the ring I had to sit on didn't provide much relief. Apart from being pleased about making a new friend and seeing a visiting physio friend who was expecting her own first child at this time, I just wanted to go home.

A couple of days later, with Lucy Anne's initial jaundice subsiding, we were free to leave. I was happy to be back home in familiar surroundings and to see the many cards and flowers that had been sent to celebrate her arrival. We had been convinced during the later stages of my pregnancy that I was carrying a boy due to my size and had decorated the second bedroom in a wallpaper sporting a pale blue sky with white clouds! The baby bouncer also had blue and white stripes on the seat.

A cuddly toy rabbit I had made sat in the bouncer and the blue carrycot part of the pram fitted into the cot perfectly. There was a selection of Babygros alongside the handknitted cardigans, shawl, mitts, bonnets and bootees in the white-painted chest of drawers. Now we had a real live baby to dress in these. It felt exciting but scary at the same time. She was all our responsibility and would be my sole responsibility when J returned to work. I didn't have any experience with new babies, or babies of any age for that matter. All I knew I had read in Miriam Stoppard's manual on childcare, which was to become my Bible in the coming months. Looking back, how I wish smartphones, Zoom calls and the internet had been available to me. It would have made a huge difference in connecting me with other new mums for support and encouragement. As it was, I felt very isolated with everyone in the flats out at work in the day except for a lovely older lady named Cath who lived on the ground floor. More about her later.

My first night home was all going swimmingly. Baby was bathed and in bed. We were all tired, and all asleep when I heard her crying. J kindly said he'd bring her in for me to breastfeed. I got ready to feed and, as he carried her into the bedroom, he promptly collapsed to the floor, falling to his left and hitting his head on the only strip of red bare floorboard in the whole room. He was knocked unconscious. I jumped out of bed at a speed that surprised me, picking up the baby who miraculously seemed unharmed and unfazed by the incident, and lay her safely in the centre of the bed.

I knelt down, hastily recalling my first aid training, and loudly spoke J's name while tapping him on the shoulders to test his responsiveness. Nothing. On looking at his chest, I could see he was still breathing, so I pulled him over into the recovery position before calling 999 for an ambulance.

I suddenly felt totally alone and very frightened. Pulling on my dressing gown, I ran to my neighbours' across the corridor and banged on the door, calling their names and asking them to help me. I hadn't realised that they'd just returned home from France with bad colds, so were reluctant at first to come over. After hearing what had happened and seeing my distress, Annette came back over with me and made us both a cup of tea while we waited for the emergency services to arrive. It was just after 2am. While I was feeding Lucy Anne, I heard a strange gurgling noise followed by a gasp and saw J was starting to come round. He opened his eyes, blinked at the bright light and saw me sitting up in bed holding the baby with Annette on the other side of the room looking out between the curtains. He looked very confused. I explained he'd collapsed and that the ambulance was on its way. They arrived shortly afterwards and took him to A&E for a check-up as this was his first collapse.

I awoke later on to the sound of his key in the door. The doctors couldn't explain why he'd collapsed but had put it down to the stress and emotion of the last few days.

Weeks passed and J returned to work. I gradually got more confident around Lucy Anne but couldn't get to grips with breastfeeding. Changing over to a bottle helped in a couple of ways: we were both more relaxed and she could take a bottle from her dad, so we could share the responsibility. One heated up the milk while the other pacified the baby. We got it down to a fine art!

I managed the practicalities of motherhood pretty well most of the time but emotionally it was a different ball game. The baby blues kicked in a few days after returning home. I remember bawling my eyes out most of the day. I didn't want to hold my baby, feed her, bath her or change her, I just wanted to go to bed and hope it was all a dream. I wanted to give her back. I was still sore when sitting and so, so tired. The bond I had with her wasn't as strong as I had expected. Nothing seemed to come naturally. I tried to learn to decipher the different cries but struggled to differentiate between the hunger cry and the dirty nappy cry, the angry cry and the tired cry. At first, I thought this was just all part of learning the ropes. That things would get easier in a few weeks.

They didn't.

I felt some days I was going mad. I could only hear crying in my head, and I couldn't stop it.

I would try to feed her, wind her, change her, rock her, play music to her, walk up and down the hall with her over my shoulder, wrap her up firmly in her blanket to help her feel secure, take her for a walk and talk to her. If she fell asleep while out in the pram she would usually wake up as soon as I got back home.

I just needed to stop, to rest, to sleep (for at least a week), to eat, to have some me time before the crying restarted. I would have benefited from noise cancelling headphones, but they didn't exist. J brought home some builder's ear protectors for me to try one day but they didn't work.

The problem wasn't the volume of her crying but the pitch. To start with I was okay, but as the cry reached a certain pitch it became unbearable, it physically hurt my ears and I just desperately wanted it to stop. I would plead with her to stop crying while trying everything I knew of to pacify her but sometimes nothing worked. I now realise she was picking up on my rising stress and anxiety because if her dad came home when she was at all distressed, she would quickly quieten down when he took over from me. This, of course, made me feel even more inadequate as a mother.

Each Friday, there was a mother and baby afternoon at the parish church. Volunteers provided tea and coffee and the local health visitor weighed and checked each baby's growth and milestones. It was my only chance to have a chat with other mums and ask what worked for them. I walked the twenty minutes there and back each week, come rain or shine, as I craved the company.

However, an hour a week wasn't enough to forge any proper friendships and I never saw any of them in the week. I did get to know one of the helpers a bit better as I saw her at the Sunday morning service most weeks. I tried to tell her how difficult I was finding it looking after Lucy Anne and how the crying affected me. I desperately needed support and help but nobody seemed to pick up on this.

Looking back a couple of years later, I realised I had postnatal depression. The crying, comfort eating, anger, frustration, extreme tiredness and lack of bonding plus the isolation were all signs that were missed. Google hadn't been invented in those days to check my symptoms and I didn't have other mums around me to ask. I just felt totally inadequate and guilty of not being good enough much of the time.

This wasn't how motherhood was meant to be. It wasn't as the books and films portrayed it. It wasn't what I had anticipated and eagerly awaited.

Yet it wasn't all bad either. Some days were better days. I enjoyed taking Lucy Anne over to play with

Hayley, who lived on the opposite side of the city and whose mum I'd met in the hospital, or to my physio friend who had her first baby shortly after me. In fact, the happy times were nearly always when I was with others, whether that was friends or the lovely old lady, Cath, in the ground-floor flat. She deserves a special mention here. I was a regular visitor to her flat. Most days I would knock on her door and she'd answer with a cigarette in her mouth. Her flat reeked of cigarette smoke, which I knew wasn't good for the baby, but she always welcomed me, made me a coffee and invited me to watch TV with her. We chatted easily about anything and everything and Lucy Anne always seemed calmer when she was there. I don't know what I would have done without her. She never realised how much I needed her, but her kindness and willingness to welcome me into her home meant the world to me.

CHAPTER 14

THE ROLLER COASTER RIDE CONTINUES

1985-1987: Aged 25-27

My maternity leave over, I was faced with a difficult decision. To return to work for the required time so as to be eligible to keep the maternity pay I had received or to stay home, forfeit that right and have to pay it all back. The thought of going to work filled me with dread, but on the other hand it could be just what I needed. It would give me time away from the flat and being a mum, plus the opportunity to regain my identity as a health professional, which in turn would help to restore my self-esteem. The decision was made for me in the end by J losing his job, not ideal from a money point of view but meaning he could take on childcare duties while I was out. It would also give him a greater understanding of how I felt looking after Lucy Anne all day. Thankfully he was a very hands-on dad, so it was decided I'd go back full time for the required time and then review the situation. The date was set. I would start back in the physiotherapy outpatient department the following week.

* * * * *

It felt like my first day. I was so nervous. The "what ifs" started to run the show in my mind. What if I couldn't remember how to conduct an assessment? What if I gave the incorrect treatment? What if I didn't fit into the team now, with so many new staff having started? So many "what ifs"!

Overthinking is a skill I have in spades. My mind whirs away as soon as a new situation arises, exploring every eventuality in an attempt to keep me firmly stuck in my comfort zone. Are you smiling? Are you an over-thinker like me? If so, let me say, the more you think, the less likely you are to take action and do the thing you want to do.

I see concepts in cartoons in my mind. I like to imagine overthinking to be like having my nose pushed up against a large boulder blocking my path. From this position I can see the boulder in GREAT detail, but nothing else. I can't see over it, round it or under it and I can't bulldoze my way through it. I can't see the bigger picture and put the boulder in perspective or see the path beyond it. I am totally and utterly stuck with my nose glued to the stone obstacle! I can't move it out of the way, even if I tried to, until I take my nose off it, step back a few paces and stop focusing on the boulder. *Then* I can see a way to get past it.

Once I overcame the initial nerves, I really enjoyed being back with the rest of my physio team. It felt good to problem solve again and see results as my patients improved with each treatment. I had missed the sense of satisfaction from being able to discharge patients who were now much better. Although I was tired when I got home from a busy day, I started to enjoy my time with Lucy Anne more and looked forward to seeing her and hearing what she and her dad had been doing. In the short term, I began to feel more like the "old me" again, the me before the baby, and this made for a happier, more relaxed family all round.

As things were getting back on an even keel, J was successful at an interview for a civil engineering role based in Aldermaston, Berkshire. The base was famous for long-running anti-nuclear CND protests around the perimeter in the eighties.

J took the job but as it was almost 100 miles away, he needed to work away through the week, just coming home for weekends. Any improvement I had made in my mental health was quickly eroded as I adapted to being effectively a single mum through the week. Weekends were eagerly anticipated, but often not as harmonious as we both expected as we had unrealistic expectations of how the weekend would go. Time was short and everything had to be crammed into a few short hours. We just started to adjust to being a family of three again when it was time to say goodbye for another week.

I've always struggled with goodbyes, as you may recall me saying when I had to catch the train back from Sheffield to college every Sunday evening. This wasn't any easier. I understand now that I suffer from a condition called "separation anxiety" when parting from someone I love. It stems from the time I was adopted and the feelings of abandonment I experienced as a baby who had been forcefully taken from her mother, and had her clothes and name changed all in one day, without being able to understand where she had gone or why this had happened. As an adult, this appears totally irrational, in that I can experience an extreme form of anxiety and fear when someone I have an emotional attachment to leaves or goes out for any reason and is heightened if they don't return at the expected time. It causes me to sob uncontrollably for a short time after they've left the house and to remain in a heightened level of anxiety until they return safe and sound. If they are later back than expected, I become increasingly worried and feel anger towards them for not contacting me to let me know they're well and why they are late.

You can imagine this anxiety added to my feeling of inadequacy as a mother was not a healthy combination for me or my child. The weekdays dragged, and I started to resent the one person in my life I was meant to love unconditionally. If it wasn't for her, I reasoned in my warped way, I wouldn't be feeling like this. I wouldn't even be in this situation. Without understanding what was happening, I sank deep into a pit of despair, developing a depression that no one saw and which I hadn't even heard of. J never knew what he would find or how I would be when he returned home. I was clingy and needy emotionally when he was around, which wasn't healthy for any of us. Something had to change and soon.

The world was such a different place back then. There was no internet to search for a home nearer to J's work or to research house prices and facilities nearby. When J wasn't actively working, he spent his time making phone calls to estate agents enquiring about two-bedroomed properties. It quickly became obvious that there was no way we could afford to live in the immediate surrounding area and so the search area grew larger and larger until he found the nearest town we *could* afford to live in, which was Swindon.

I hadn't heard anything good about Swindon. The impression I had was an industrial town with little to recommend it apart from its links to Isambard Kingdom Brunel. The estate agents posted the particulars of what they considered to be suitable properties.

Eventually, a two-bedroomed end-terrace house with a small garden in a quiet cul-de-sac close to local amenities turned up. It was located on the outskirts of Swindon in an area imaginatively called West Swindon, but most importantly, it was within budget.

J was able to view it on his way back from work

one Friday and I trusted his judgement. They say beggars can't be choosers and I was desperate to move somewhere within easy commuter distance, so J could get home each night. This would be our first family home.

On moving day, it rained heavily with a cascade of water pouring off the removal van roof throughout the day. However, that was a small price to pay for being able to be together each day.

Another advantage of living on the outskirts of Swindon was both sets of parents were able to visit and see their granddaughter on a regular basis. I was also able to drive over to see my mum when I needed extra company or support.

I quickly unpacked and settled in, making new friends with the other young families around me. One single mum in particular, who lived across the street, made a special effort to welcome and befriend me. I soon became a regular visitor to her home for a cuppa, a piece of cake and a chat while Lucy Anne played happily alongside her young son. She invited me to her church that met in the school hall just a few minutes' walk away, and I enjoyed meeting more young mums there. I got on particularly well with Helen, a fellow physio who I met there with a daughter the same age as Lucy Anne. The girls got on like a house on fire. We met up several times a week for lunch and a play date. I quickly discovered three local playgrounds, all less than thirty minutes' walk away, and Helen introduced me to a mums and toddler group in the next-door area of West Swindon. It was a perfect spot to raise children. There was even a leisure centre with a swimming pool and ice rink on the doorstep. I was supported on every side, which made a huge difference, but I still struggled with bouts of low mood that descended on me without warning and were hard to shift. I wasn't officially diagnosed as having PND (postnatal depression) until my initial onboarding appointment with the local surgery when I was finally given a name for this thing that was blighting my life as a new mother. There was relief in knowing I wasn't imagining it and being prescribed my first pack of antidepressants.

As anyone who has experienced depression will be aware, it takes a few weeks for the medication to start to take effect and there are always side effects. One of the most common one is weight gain – just what I didn't want as I was struggling to lose my baby weight. However, I accepted this in the hope that my emotions would start to feel more balanced. It took a few tweaks in dosage to get the desired effect but finally I started to function better without dissolving into tears or getting irritable at the slightest thing.

It wasn't a quick fix, far from it, but with the love and friendship of those around, my newfound Christian faith and church family supporting us, life started to contain more good days than bad with periods of joy and happiness.

I returned part time at Princess Margaret's

Hospital two days a week, based in the outpatient physio department. Nine months later, I discovered I was expecting my second child. Due to the postnatal depression after Lucy Anne, I was offered the support of a Home Start volunteer, Penny, from nearby Ashton Keynes. We hit it off straight away and formed a firm friendship before Jane, my second daughter, made her appearance in April 1987.

The birth was very different from my first. It was traumatic for a completely different reason. It was thought, in hindsight, she had spun round, causing the cord to become caught around her neck when my waters broke shortly after I was induced. This wasn't known at the time, so when I was pushing hard to no avail, the cord was, in fact, strangling her. Once the midwife noticed her little blue face and felt the cord around her neck, she quickly cut it, freeing her before pulling her out at some speed. I had my eyes screwed shut at that point, as I felt her little body being wrenched out of me. J, however, had seen her blueish body before they whisked her away, leaving us alone in the delivery room, not knowing what was happening. I was confused. I wanted them to stitch me up and wondered where everyone had gone. J started to cry. When I asked him what the matter was, he told me she was blue and not breathing when she was born, and she'd been taken away to try to revive her. It seemed an eternity before the midwife returned holding what appeared to be a square piece of thick paper in her hand. She handed it to me. It was a square Polaroid photograph of my baby lying in an incubator. Someone had written the words "baby (my surname) 9lb" at the bottom. We had decided on first and middle names for a girl or a boy a few weeks before. The girl's names were Jane Hannah. As Hannah derives from the Hebrew Channah meaning grace, it seemed even more fitting now, as by the grace of God she had survived. The staff told us she'd needed support to breathe and had started to fit from lack of oxygen, but had begun to breathe on her own just before the ten minute deadline (when they declare a baby to be stillborn). She was certainly a miracle baby.

Due to her being deprived of oxygen for a period of time, the special care doctors were concerned she may have cerebral palsy. This news came as a huge shock. I hadn't given a thought to the possible long-term effects of her difficulties at birth. I was concentrating on the fact she was alive and somehow survived.

The church family were a great support to us all, setting up a prayer chain, delivering meals to our door each day and offering childminding so Lucy Anne could stay with a friend while her dad visited Jane and myself in the SCBU (special care baby unit).

Mum drove over the next day to see her newest grandchild attached to monitors on every side in her incubator. She was allowed to slide her fingers in through the side opening to hold Jane's hand. We asked a nurse to take a photo. It was a special moment. I can see it in my mind's eye as I write.

A second miracle occurred three days after her birth. The monitor and tubes were gone, and she lay in a clear plastic hospital cot touching the top with her head and the bottom with her toes. Up to this point, she had been fed remotely, but it was decided, as I had wanted to breastfeed her, to give it a try. I was warned she may have lost the sucking reflex as it hadn't been stimulated since being born. There was no comparison with my previous experience. I had a nurse beside me, who was gentle and sensitive in her approach. She listened to my past memories of failure around breastfeeding Lucy Anne, and encouraged me, giving practical guidance on how best to hold Jane for her to easily "latch on". Neither of us could believe our eyes. She had no difficulty sucking effectively. It was a triumph for us both. I was asked to use a breast pump once I was discharged from the postnatal ward, tipping the collected milk into small glass bottles, which I labelled and took in for them to use overnight.

The Sunday after Jane's birth was Easter and also my birthday. The weather was warm, and the house and garden filled with flowers. I love the springtime, and especially the bright yellow of the daffodils. They always bring a smile to my face. This was indeed a unique birthday for me. I had taken in some first-size baby dresses borrowed from a friend the previous day. When I arrived at the hospital, Jane looked so beautiful dressed in a cream and dusky pink flowered dress with a white collar. The SCBU nurses had thoughtfully taped a note to the head of her baby cot that read "Happy Birthday, Mum!"

Lucy Anne, now aged just over two and a half, had come with us that morning, bringing a small soft toy present for her new sister and a line drawing in dark pink felt-tip pen of her, which we secured by tucking it down the side of the mini cot mattress.

All the initial tests came back clear, and things were looking hopeful. There were no further signs of fitting or other brain disturbance over the following days, so Jane was discharged home after a week.

The weather continued to be more like summer than spring, warm enough to sit out watching Lucy Anne playing in the garden while the baby slept in her pram.

Not being isolated in a first-floor flat this time, I found things easier and enjoyed being able to wheel the pram round the block to visit friends or go to the supermarket, calling at the swings on the way. Penny remained in touch for another year, and even had Jane to stay one time when she was teething to give us a good night's sleep. It was a great loss and shock when I received a call to say she had sadly been severely injured in a road traffic incident. She survived the crash but wasn't able to walk, having suffered brain damage. I joined her friends and family in praying for her healing on a warm summer's eve and later on visited her when she was discharged home. It made me keenly aware of how fragile life is. I will never forget the support and friendship she gave me. I believe the fact that my depression didn't return at this point was in part due to her being in our lives.

CHAPTER 15

FAMILY LIFE'S UPS AND DOWNS

Age 29-42: 1988-2002

Two small children in a family means life is never predictable but also life is never boring.

There were milestones to measure and celebrate, ink marks on the kitchen doorpost to mark their growth spurts, charts to tick off the daily tasks and the favourite penny chart. I came across this idea in one of many parenthood books I consulted on a regular basis called *Dare to Discipline*. The concept of rewarding good, kind and helpful behaviour isn't new and I had always rewarded single acts of kindness at the time they happened. I verbally praised the girls when they were kind to each other or were helpful but hadn't thought of chalking these good turns up on a weekly chart. I wrote a selection of positive actions I wanted to reinforce on the left-hand side and the days of the week along the top of the chart. Some of the actions worthy of a tick on the chart were:

- Putting toys away.
- Helping to lay the table.
- Saying "please".
- Saying "thank you".
- Showing kindness to one another.
- Helping me dust the lounge.
- Putting their dirty clothes in the wash basket.

Simple things, generally helping the girls to act in a caring and helpful way. At the end of the week, the ticks were totalled up and they earnt that amount in 1p coins.

This was very popular with them both as they looked forward to choosing a small treat, such as a small pack of crayons, chocolate, a toy or small game from a colourful biscuit tin kept on top of the kitchen units. These ranged from 5p to 20p and aimed to help them grasp the concept of paying for things or saving up for a more expensive 20p treat.

I love nature and enjoy creative activities, so I was in my element, introducing the girls to the flora and fauna around the area, from tadpoles in the stream to tiny insects in the garden. They were, as most young children are, inquisitive and excited by anything that moved. We counted spots on ladybirds and made glass bottle homes for caterpillars, watching them chomp through the leaves and grow bigger by the day. I've always loved butterflies and so delighted in taking the girls to a butterfly farm and local wildlife park. We bought an annual pass as every school holiday saw us packing up a picnic and heading down to Burford to enjoy a day of penguin, monkey, tiger, camel and hippo watching, along with zebras and many other creatures great and small. These visits always ended in the shop and discussions as to what to buy with their pocket money, usually erasers, rulers, fridge magnets and pencils being the most commonly chosen items. My love of stationery obviously rubbed off on them!

There were so many happy days, more than I had remembered until writing this chapter. Weekends had a regular routine of a visit to the local country park and lake with the accompanying tears from trips and falls off slides and climbing equipment.

I recall frantic cries one afternoon from Lucy Anne, whose baby tooth had come out and dropped on the safety bark below the wooden climbing structure. Have you ever looked for a needle in a haystack? I couldn't believe my luck when, as I was about to give up, I saw a white spot shining in the sun a few inches away from where I was looking. Relief flowed through me as I picked up the milk tooth that would be placed under my daughter's pillow that night to be exchanged for a twenty pence piece by the kindly tooth fairy!

As well as fun outings to parks and play areas, we began to develop a less pleasurable pattern of visits to the local accident and emergency department. Lucy Anne loved playing out with the other children in the street, predominantly boys who tore up and down the road on their bikes as part of their imaginary play. I was regularly faced with her friends rushing into the house to tell me, in an urgent tone, that she had fallen off her bike and was bleeding or otherwise needing my attention. Out came the disinfectant and cotton wool, the soothing cream and plasters I kept on standby. Often this was sufficient to mend the injured soldier, but on several occasions the damage was more than I could fix, so a trip to the hospital was needed.

After the first couple of times, I had a mental list of what to take with us. A few drinks and snacks, a small toy to play with, a puzzle book and pencil, tissues and purse with coins for the payphone if needed. I used to joke with the staff about us having reserved seats, not realising at the time how this might have looked to them.

Three times she fractured a little bone in her hand that is notorious for not healing and doesn't always show up on X-ray until ten days after the initial injury. It's called the scaphoid and is located in an area colourfully named the anatomical snuff box, at the base of the thumb. The fourth injury, following a spectacular bike accident, was a fractured medial epicondyle of her right elbow, the knob of bone you feel on the inside of your elbow that is the point of attachment for a muscle on your forearm and around which nerves run. It is therefore sometimes a problematic fracture. The timing couldn't have been worse for us as we were heading to Disneyland Paris – a special Easter present from my mum – a day or so afterwards, with Lucy Anne now in an elbow plaster and sling, making dressing and sleeping difficult. However, it turned out to be a real advantage for her as all the Disney characters made a beeline to sign her plaster, much to her younger sister's annoyance. We kept that cast for many years as a souvenir of her trip – no pun intended!

* * * * *

Family life, with its ups and downs, joys and trials, was in full swing. In that way, we were no different than any other family. Yet under the surface and behind closed doors, things weren't quite as they seemed. The postnatal depression with its emotional swings stayed with me through these early years with the girls. It could turn me from loving mum to an angry person in the blink of an eye, which was distressing for all concerned. I continued to seek help and support for this from different sources, including a well-respected Christian counsellor recommended to me by a close friend.

These sessions proved as illuminating as they were helpful. I worked through the emotional aftereffects of my adoption and was able to uncover and explore the guilt and shame I carried from my decision to have the termination as a teenager. I could see my current postnatal depression was in part linked to the sense of abandonment, lost-ness and frustration I had experienced at the start of my life. The loneliness of being an only child who didn't feel she fitted in linked to the seeming inability to be the perfect mother I felt I ought to be, serene and unruffled by the dramas of everyday life, as pictured in some idyllic yesteryear family portrait. Always smiling and gracious, with a sweet temper and boundless patience to easily deal with whatever transpired. This was the image I was comparing myself to, an impossible standard, which resulted in self-loathing and anger that turned in on itself becoming depression. Why do we do this to ourselves? Set up a standard that is way beyond our human reach.

Looking back, I had always been striving to be someone I wasn't. The perfect daughter, intellectual, achieving top grades at everything she turned her hand to, a socially acceptable creature accepted and loved by all she encountered; a girl who attracted the cream of the crop in the area of suitors and married above her station or at least to someone well respected by her parents and peers. A competent housewife, versed in home management and known for her culinary prowess and the perfect, well-balanced mother of two adorable, well-behaved children.

This was my standard.

To write this shocks me, even now. Never had I realised how impossible a task I had set myself. No wonder I felt I was failing on so many levels!

To address the buried trauma and past pain, I wrote

letters of forgiveness, which I would repeat later in my life as I peeled back the next layer of this particular onion. I wrote forgiving my birth mother for giving me up for adoption, for unintentionally abandoning me. I wrote forgiving my adoptive parents for not meeting my needs to be held, to be understood, to be valued for who I was (rather than be compared to others, resulting in a sense of lack on my part for not being who they wanted me to be). I wrote telling them how this had made me feel. None of these letters were sent, just written as a way of expressing things that needed to be said.

More letters, more recently, have been written to my younger teenage self, forgiving her for the decisions she made under pressure, for the effect her actions had on those around her, for the way her decision deprived her unborn child of the right to live. These words, in total honesty, are painful to pen, even today. None of us can change one stroke of our past. All we can do is examine it, and attempt to understand it with the reasons and emotions surrounding it. Then forgive and let go. To hold on is to continue to berate ourselves for something we can never change. To hold on does nothing but stifle our ability to move on. To learn and to take inspired action is to live a better future.

Be kind to yourself as you would to another soul who unburdened themselves to you. Be gentle and understanding to your younger self. Forgive your past mistakes, knowing that every person on earth gets it wrong sometimes, and turn those mistakes into something that you can be proud of, something that will help others avoid the pitfalls you encountered.

I believe there is no greater thing than this, to walk alongside another on their journey, having the understanding of your own.

This is my desire in my writing. My passion and my quest to reach others who are sinking or who have a secret that is eating them up and to say, "I see you, and I have good news, there is a route *out* from a place called Shame."

ACKNOWLEDGMENTS

Many people have been instrumental in supporting and encouraging me through the trials and tribulations recounted in this book. Too many to list by name. To you all I extend my sincere thanks.

In particular, I thank my heavenly adoptive parents Jill and Barry. You both gave me the best you were able. A safe space in which to grow up, a good education and the opportunity to explore my musical talents, following in my grandma's footsteps in the realms of the piano playing and singing.

I am grateful for the charity NORCAP who enabled me to trace my birth families, leading to me finding my roots, discovering who I really am and the circumstances around my beginnings. I am very thankful for the warm welcomes both families have given me. I now know who I am and that I am loved and accepted by my mum and dad in a way I hadn't experienced prior to finding them.

Next, I want to acknowledge my first husband, J, and my two daughters. We shared so much happiness over the twenty-four years we were together. You loved me, treated me with respect and tried your hardest to understand and alleviate my gremlins. For these things I will always be grateful.

I've come across some amazing friends along my path who have laughed and cried with me, listened without judgment and cared. Among these, I particularly want to thank Kathy and Dawn from my college days and Helen and Liz in my days as a young and often overwhelmed young mother. Hayley, Christine, Irene and Sue, who stuck by me when many others deserted me as my world appeared to fall apart. Without you, I'm not sure I would have made it through the emotional turmoil.

Thinking more recently, I thank Mary, Liz, Carol, Louise and my MLM friends for being there for me and introducing me to the concepts of mindset and personal development. This was a game changer for me. It gave me a framework and method by which I could restore my self-belief one affirmation at a time. I was able to identify the old stories that were holding me back and begin to discover a new positive future. As I'm writing this, "One Day Over the Rainbow" is playing in the café... so apt!

My heartfelt thanks also go to my personal coach Tracey who has helped me to identify and tussle with the monsters from my past, and my friend and fellow author Cassandra Welford, whose willingness to share her journey inspired me to write my own. Thank you, Cassie, and all the Writing Academy members, for your ongoing support. You are my cheerleaders and I am yours.

Finally, my thanks go to my fellow entrepreneurs, business mentors and everyone involved in the publishing process of *From a Place Called Shame*. Finally, a very special thank you to Jen Parker of Fuzzy Flamingo. Your guidance through the twists and turns of this process has been priceless.

"It always seems impossible until it is done."
Author unknown

TAKING IT FURTHER

Introduction

One reason behind me putting pen to paper and telling my story was to turn taboo topics into talking points.

To facilitate this, I have created five "Talking Points" suitable for individual study or small group discussion to further the reader's awareness of their own values and beliefs in these areas and foster greater insight and empathy (in place of judgement) in those who find themselves spectators or in close contact with others travelling these challenging paths. Each Talking Point is linked to the relevant chapter and page and looks at a different topic.

I strongly believe that, when we are prepared to set aside our preconceptions to really listen and hear another's experience, we grow in our understanding and the way we perceive the world.

I envision a comfortable, relaxed setting with a small group gathered with light refreshments, pens, notebooks and tissues on hand!

You may be in a school, college or university setting. You may be a group of young mums or a book group. You may be a teen, single parent or grandparent, a teacher or a counsellor, or any other profession or none.

These subjects affect every strata and section of community, every nation and most family histories.

They have been buried for far too long and the shame they create has stifled and at times snuffed out too many lives. My hope and desire is, for the coming together of groups all around the globe, both virtually and in person, to be open, to listen, to hear, to discuss, to assess and re-evaluate their own beliefs and to reach out with a new and genuine compassion to the misunderstood, the hurting, the damaged ones amongst and around them.

FIVE STUDIES TO CHALLENGE YOUR POINT OF VIEW

TALKING POINT 1: New Start, New Feelings

Chapters 2-3

Before you start: Agree some group boundaries and rules.

It helps to ask the group what they would like to include and write them up so everyone can see them. Some suggestions are:

1. What is said in the room, stays in the room.
2. Listen to who is speaking without interruption.
3. Have an open-minded attitude to hear what others are saying, etc.

Introduction

These chapters talk of my three years at Physiotherapy School and my first experience of living away from home, at the age of eighteen.

My expectations of this period of time were very different from the reality. I had expected to have a great social life alongside my studies. In actual fact, there was almost no social life linked with my college friends.

Whether you are at school, college, university or work, or none of these settings, you may, at times, have experienced feelings of isolation or anxiety.

This section looks at these feelings, the reasons around them and ways we can deal with them.

Icebreakers

• Think of a time you started something new. Share with the group what this new activity was and what emotions came up for you at the start of this time. Write the key emotions on a whiteboard or large sheet of paper.

Or

• I describe feeling alone/isolated when the rest of my year group went home at weekends.

Have you ever had a situation when you felt this way?

Group questions

1. Why do you think uncomfortable emotions surface when you start a new venture?
2. How has your experience of starting a new job/school/social group, etc. been affected by your mindset (the beliefs we have about life)?
3. What beliefs do you have around making a new start? E.g.: No one will like me/I'm no good with new things/I love meeting new people, etc. Make a note of these.

For this next section divide into small groups of 2-3

1. Now you've identified this mind chatter (the thoughts and beliefs around new starts that you've shared in the group), ask yourself these questions about each belief that you are aware of :
   a. Where did this belief originate?
   b. When did I first think this?
   c. Who told me this?

Make a note of your answers for future reference. Share one of these with your small group buddy.

Author Note

These beliefs are just something you've collected over time, and many will go back to childhood. Once you understand that they're not necessarily true, just something you absorbed when you were too young to challenge what others said to you and that your brain has accepted, *you can start the process of changing them to more helpful and empowering beliefs. Here is how…*

2. Start by thinking of a word or phrase that is *opposite* to the belief that comes up most often for you from the list you've written down. (Ask your group buddy for help if you can't think of anything.)

It needs to be a positive word, phrase or sentence starting with I am… I can… etc.

Here are some examples:
*   I am liked and accepted by those who meet me.
*   I love to try new things.
*   I'm looking forward to enjoying new activities.

3. Choose one of your phrases. Write it somewhere you will see it several times in the day.
    −   You could write a note or reminder on your phone or make it your screensaver.
    −   You could write it on a card stuck on a mirror or cupboard.

Where will you put it? Chat to your group buddy about your choice.

4. To change how we think after years of negative reinforcement needs persistence. Keep challenging your old beliefs by speaking out the new ones… that remind your brain how you would like to think and feel.

Commit today to speaking your new belief *out loud,* if possible (as your brain believes what you tell it), several times a day. I like to do this while waiting for the kettle to boil.

You may like to be accountable to your group buddy and support each other in your resolve to change those negative beliefs one day at a time.

Optional extra discussion questions

You may like to suggest group members look at these and bring their thoughts back to the next meeting. There is also an opportunity to look at these in Talking Point 5.

Stress and coping strategies

1. We all have different ways – coping strategies, as I call them – to manage difficult emotions. Mine was to run away from college (chapter 8). How do *you* manage emotions of anxiety / inadequacy / uncertainty / fear?

2. Can you think of a *better* way I could have dealt with my feelings of unhappiness in year two?
3. Look at one of *your* coping strategies, what you do when you are upset, angry or stressed. How else could you respond?
4. How might you recognise someone who is struggling with their feelings?
5. What could you do to help?

To Close:

Come back together into your main group.

Give time for members to share one thing that has helped them or they have learnt from this Talking Point

**The group leader may like to remind everyone of the need for confidentiality before the group leaves **

TALKING POINT 2: Changing Times, Changing Opinions

Chapter 2 and 4-5

Remind the group of the agreed rules and boundaries from the first study

Introduction

My opinions and beliefs around the subject of teenage pregnancy changed radically when I found myself in that very situation.

Ice breakers

- When have you experienced a 360-degree change of heart or viewpoint in your life?

Or

- What difference does it make seeing a situation from the inside, rather than as a spectator?

Break into twos or threes for the next few discussion questions. It would be helpful to change who you buddy up with, so you hear a different perspective each time you meet.

Remember: try to put *your own* opinion to one side as you listen to your group buddy.

1. Identify 3-5 ways you might gain a better understanding of how it looks and feels to be a teenage girl who discovers she's pregnant or who has been raped or taken advantage of in some way.

2. **Pause and Reflect** on your thoughts, words and actions in the past towards others who find themselves in challenging situations.
   a. Did you avoid them or cut them off while they were talking?
   b. Did you listen or try to fix them?
   c. Is there anyone you owe an apology to, or you will speak more kindly to, in the future? Make a note in your notebook or in your phone calendar to do this.

3. Discuss how you would like to be treated if you were in this situation or any situation where you felt hurt and upset.

4. Remind yourself of my experience of rape in Chapter 2 and coming to a decision whether to go

ahead with the termination in Chapters 4-5
a. Do you see things any differently now?
b. If so, in what way?
c. How do you feel?
d. Share one positive change you will make when you hear about someone who is facing a difficult situation.

To Close:

Come back together in your group and give each small group or pair the opportunity to give feedback on what they've learnt about themselves through this Talking Point.

**The group leader may like to remind everyone of the need for confidentiality before the group leaves **

TALKING POINT 3: Decisions, Decisions

Chapters 5-6

Recall your group rules and boundaries

Introduction

At some times in life, we are faced with what may seem to be an impossible decision. A decision of such magnitude that we squirm at the consequences of our choice, whichever way we jump. Add time pressure, religious beliefs and conflicting peer and professional advice and you've got an extremely stressful situation.

As a practicing Christian and an adoptee, my beliefs were very definite: abortion was wrong. Full stop. Little did I imagine I would be in a position of having to make a choice between having a termination or going down the route to adoption.

Ice Breakers:

* Do you know anyone who is adopted or had a termination?

— **Without identifying them**, explain how this influenced your thoughts and beliefs on this subject.

Or

- Use your phone to research and discover which countries in the world consider abortion to be illegal.
  — How do you think these differences affect people's thoughts and feelings around this subject?

Group activity

Divide a large piece of paper or whiteboard into two columns. Head the left column Adoption and the right one Abortion/Termination.

Ask the group to add reasons to support each choice in the case of an unplanned pregnancy.

To help you start, I've given you a possible suggestion below.

Adoption	Abortion/Termination
I was adopted	Fear of rejection
Possible contact later in life	Need to complete college

In your small group

1. I described the time between a positive pregnancy test result (in my day this was at the surgery) and the procedure using words such as:
    — Strained
    — Nervous
    — Scared
    — Uncertain
    — Ashamed
    a. What external and environmental pressures did I face?
    b. What internal conflicts do I identify?
    c. Which of these would be relevant if you or a friend of yours were in a similar situation?
    d. Can you identify any other factors that would either add or ease the stress experienced by someone in this position in your country today?

2. Where would you advise a friend to go for in-person or online support and guidance?
   — Do you have any support groups or sources of advice close to where you live?

3. **Reflection**: If this happened to you, who would you talk to, who would you trust?
   — You may like to keep a journal of your thoughts and feelings through the next few weeks to share next time you meet up with the group.

To Close:

Return as a full group and share in one word how you are feeling.

Remind the group of the group agreement re confidentiality and offer to help access support for any group member who has found this Talking Point upsetting.

Note: There are suggestions of online sources of support in Appendix 3.

TALKING POINT 4: Motherhood, best time of your life or mental health nightmare?

Chapters 12-14

Remind the group of the agreed rules and boundaries

Introduction

This time I was really looking forward to my pregnancy and being the proud mum I had always dreamed of being. Yet, like most things in life, the reality turned out to be rather different to the Disney version!

Ice Breakers:

- What images and words does the word *motherhood* evoke?
- Make a visual collection of these on your whiteboard or piece of paper.

OR

- Type the words mother, mum and motherhood

into a search engine on your phone.

- What images come up?
- What do these convey about motherhood?

Group activity

Share emotions and beliefs you have, or you have heard from family or friends, around being a mum. Notice how varied or similar these are.

- What part does age and culture play in the way mothers are perceived?
- Are mothers thought of differently across the globe?
- Are there any common ideas around motherhood that unite all mothers everywhere?

Being the first in my work team to go on maternity leave meant I had a few months leading up to the birth when I felt isolated and left out. All of a sudden, I wasn't part of the gang.

Can you relate to this at all?

In your small group

1. What kinds of antenatal support are available where you live?
   a. Is there anything that would improve the

      experience of expectant or new mothers in your locality?

b. If you have some ideas or other feedback, take this time to draft out a short email to the head of maternity services in your local NHS trust (UK), or other organisation.

c. Start by outlining areas where care is good and effective and then go onto positive ideas for change to better the service.

2. The overwhelm that hit me on my return home from the hospital with my baby (Chapter 13) was totally unexpected.
   — What could be done to minimise these feelings in a new mum?

3. Reread chapter 13. List the symptoms of postnatal depression that I struggled with.
   — No one suggested I had PND (postnatal depression) at the time.
   — Why do you think it was missed?

4. When, in April 1987, I gave birth to my second daughter (Chapter 14), I had been concerned about the depression returning. Despite the traumatic nature of the birth, it didn't in the same way. Why do you think this was?

Reflection

- Take a few minutes to be still.
- Think about your own circumstances, if you have children. Look at your thinking and behaviour patterns.

Note: If you struggle with extreme tiredness, tearfulness, irritability, lack of appetite or sleep, or any other symptoms that have started since you became pregnant or became a mum, please speak to someone you trust, your health visitor, midwife or doctor. There are many forms of support and treatment available for mental health concerns during and after childbirth. No one will judge you.

You won't be the first or the last to need a chat either to reassure you or refer you to a professional that can help.

To close:

I found friendships with other mums with similar aged children made a big difference to my confidence and day-to-day ability to cope with two young children. If your group has young mums in it, ask if anyone would like to meet up between the group sessions for a cuppa and chat or if they would like to set up a support/chat group on a messaging platform.

Be aware of the need for child-friendly venues and to be mindful of GDPR when sharing numbers to set a group up.

TALKING POINT 5: Family, childhood and other bits and bobs

Chapter 15

Remind the group of the agreed rules and boundaries

Introduction

The phrase "family life" conjures up a myriad of images, words and memories, not all of them positive or happy. I do understand this. As with the other talking points, we need to be kind and caring when we listen to each other.

Ice Breaker

- There are many definitions of family these days. Make a list of some of these that you are part of or aware of.

OR

- What shapes our understanding of the phrase family life?

- As a group, make your own definition of the word family in a few sentences.

In your small group

1. Being an only adopted child and the youngest in my secondary school year meant that I was very naïve and often felt an outsider. Being constantly compared to a very bright daughter of my parents' bridge friends meant I grew up feeling I was **never** quite good enough.
   — Can you relate to or understand these feelings?

Either:

If you are a parent:

- Do you see yourself doing this and how can you ensure your child knows they are always enough?

OR

If this is you:

- Please believe me that you are **SO** GOOD ENOUGH, no matter what has been said to you at any time by anyone else. It may help to talk to an adult you trust, a counsellor or a helpline (see Appendix 3) about your emotions around this.

— *You are certainly not the only person who has felt this way. You can turn things around as I did to start to believe in yourself again.*

Look back at the group work on "Coping Strategies" from Talking Point 1. There is an optional section you may like to do at this point.

In Chapter 15, I recall some of the good memories of my own children together with some of the challenges for them and for myself.

Spend a few minutes searching your memory banks for the happy times with your "family", however you define that concept.

To close:

Allow the group to enjoy sharing one or two of these happy memories.

CONCLUSIONS

When your group has completed the five Talking Point studies, use these prompts to facilitate a full group discussion.

Discuss as a group

- Have your feelings and opinions altered as you've shared and listened to the experiences and thoughts of others?
- If so, share with the group what made a difference to your thinking and how you feel now.

What will you do differently?

This is a great time to set personal intentions moving forward.
- What will you do differently from now?
- Who will you treat differently?
- How will you support friends or others you meet in the future?

AND FINALLY

If you just change **one** thing you think, believe or do as a result of reading my story and hearing others' stories in your group then my purpose of writing will have been achieved and my vulnerability worthwhile.

Every small change in your thoughts leads to a change in your beliefs, actions and behaviour.

Reflection

Each person who gains a deeper and wider understanding creates a ripple of understanding in those around them (who witness a change in how they speak or act).

Each person who cares more starts a ripple of compassion.

Each person who reaches out to someone and listens empathetically leads to a ripple of love and acceptance.

How will you start a ripple today?

SELF-HELP SUGGESTIONS

I have created a helpful PDF for anyone who's felt the impact of the life experiences I have shared in this book.

It contains six specific personal development tools and tips that took me from being a prisoner to my past to embracing my flaws and developing a healthy self-image.

Six Simple Steps to Shift the Shame can be found here:

https://www.subscribepage.com/6-simple-steps-to-shift-the-shame_copy

Psychodynamic and other forms of counselling all played a part in my recovery journey, as did my local MIND support group and various medications. However, there was still inner work to be done to address the real deep-rooted causes of my constant desire to be liked, needed, accepted, recognised and validated.

- Maybe you are there too?
- Maybe you get frustrated at the way that you never quite make it?
- Maybe you think others are always better than you and you don't have what is needed to succeed or set big goals?
- Maybe you are tired of feeling disappointed when you don't win the prize or get the promotion?
- Maybe you are still beating yourself up for messing up in the past?
- Maybe you are still wearing an invisible cloak of shame that prevents you from stepping into the limelight?

Does this resonate? If so, I am writing this with you in mind, because this is **exactly** where I was back in 2013.

Those of you who have read my chapter, Little Miss Misunderstood (chapter 1 of the collaborative book *Beautifully Broken*) will have some insight into how my wounded inner child had an impact on my life.

Beautifully Broken is available on Amazon here: https://amzn.to/3Rt32dW

However, my self-improvement journey really began in earnest in 2019, after signing up with a network marketing business helping people save money on their everyday bills. Everyone in my team told me success was linked to having a growth mindset and taking time on personal development.

What was this mindset thing?

Personal what?

I had so many questions!

My team leaders recommended podcasts and books that clearly explained these two subjects, which were totally new to me, starting with the basics. I've listed a few at the end of this chapter.

As a newcomer, I was keen to be the best I could be and so began the slow, day by day turning of the Titanic. I began to learn and understand for the first time how my brain functioned, why I was stuck in a repeating cycle of never quite reaching my goal and never *quite* being good enough, in my reckoning. I discovered tools to manage anxiety and fear. I found ways to combat the overwhelm and imposter syndrome that would stop me in my tracks – the inner voices that would tell me I wasn't good enough and would defeat me before I even stepped foot out of my comfort zone.

At last, I had found the keys I had been searching for all my life to unlock my true potential and shift the needle where confidence and self-belief were concerned.

Don't get me wrong, like learning any new skill, I would have breakthroughs followed by a slip back. Yet when I look back to the woman I was in 2019, I hardly recognise her. The frustrated, tearful and easily defeated me has been transformed to one who constantly steps out of her comfort zone to try new things and speaks up rather than stays quiet, as this book shows. Yes, I still have areas that need work, it's a lifetime's work, but the difference is I now *know* and have *proved* that the time I spend on personal development is worth it, powerful and effective. It has made a very real difference, borne out by the many lovely encouraging comments from my fellow authors and entrepreneurs over the past three years.

I sincerely hope these simple, yet effective tips and ideas boost **your** self-image as they did mine.

Here is the free link again:

https://www.subscribepage.com/6-simple-steps-to-shift-the-shame_copy

I'd also love to hear your stories and wins, as you incorporate these life-enhancing tools into your daily life.

You can message me here:

carolyn.parker@restoringselfbelief.co.uk

I look forward to hearing from you. I read every message, which, as you will appreciate can take some time, so it may take me a few days to reply.

As promised earlier, here are a few of the many inspirational books that helped me turn my life around.

Books :

Daring Greatly: Brené Brown
Rising Strong: Brené Brown
The Secret: Rhonda Byrne
The Alchemist: Paulo Coelho
Quiet: Fearne Cotton
Good Vibes, Good Life: Vex King
The Self-Care Project: Jayne Hardy

Podcasts:

Unlocking Us: Brené Brown
Limitless Life: Melyssa Griffin
How To Be A Better Human: Chris Duffy
7 Good Minutes: Clyde Lee Dennis
The Overwhelmed Brain: Paul Colaini

I end this section with one of my favourite quotes written by Daniell Koepk (in *Daring to Take Up Space*):

"You don't have to solve your whole life overnight. And you don't have to feel ashamed for being who you are. All you have to focus on is one small thing that you can do **today** *to get closer to where you want to be. Slowly and lightly, one step at a time. You can get there."*

SOURCES OF SUPPORT AND FURTHER INFORMATION

Here is a selection of general resources that may give updated information and extra support. As I was researching these, I came across many regional sources of advice and support, which obviously differ depending on where you live. You can find details of what's going on locally from your surgery website, library, wellbeing centre, council, church, voluntary hub, etc.

If you are using my book with a group, you may like to collect and print a selection of your own local support services to distribute to your group members.

Disclaimer

By listing these organisations, I am not recommending them. I have used some of these resources, but not all of them, so they are suggestions rather than recommendations.

Support in Pregnancy

NHS
Confidential Advice from a GP, practice nurse, sexual health or contraceptive clinic and by calling 111.
https://www.nhs.uk

Tommy's
A website led by midwives giving up-to-date information for parents to be.
www.tommys.org.uk

Brook
Under-25's advice in pregnancy and after birth.
https://www.brook.org.uk

Family Nurse Partnership
Support from a family nurse visiting your home from early pregnancy until your child is two years old.
https://fro.nhs.uk

Mental Health Support in Pregnancy

Maternal Mental Health Alliance
Crisis Support.
https://maternalmentalhealthalliance.org

Kids Health
Mental Health care for parents in pregnancy.
https://kidshealth.org

MIND
Peri and postnatal mental health including how to cope while pregnant and with a young baby.
https://mind.org.uk

Support Networks for parents
(including those who support those experiencing postnatal mental health concerns)

Family Lives
Support for families and young parents.
0808 800 2222
https://www.familylives.org.uk

Little Lullaby
Online support network for young parents to chat, share advice and stories.
https://littlelullaby.org.uk

Best Beginnings
Supporting all parents, co-parents and caregivers to give their children the best beginning in life.
They run the free Baby Buddy App endorsed by the Department of Health.
https://bestbeginnings.org

PANDAS email support
Available 365 days a year. Responds within 72 hours.
Info@pandasfoundation.org.uk

Shelter
Housing advice and support.
https://shelter.org

MIND
Three videos, the first free and two aimed at facilitating businesses to provide work-based support for parents.
www.parentinginmind.com

Adoption Support/Information

Information on the adoption process and legalities around who can adopt and be adopted, including overseas adoption.
https://www.gov.uk/childcare-parenting/adoption-fostering-and-surrogacy

Banardos
The UK's largest voluntary adoption agency.
https://banardos.org

First4Adoption
The national adoption information service for England.
https://first4adoption.org

ICA Centre
The only UK international adoption centre.
https://icacentre.org

Adoption UK
Support, advice, friendship and resources for people touched by adoption. Weekly virtual meet ups, community support groups across the UK and webinars full of information, experience and knowledge.
https://adoption.uk.org

Counselling Support

SANDS
The Stillbirth and Neonatal Death Society. Support for anyone following the death of a baby.
www.sands.org.uk

BACP (British Association for Counselling and Psychotherapy)
A professional association with over 50,000 members in the UK promoting the role and relevance of counselling in improving psychological well-being and mental health and developing safe, ethical and competent practice.
https://bacp.co.uk

UKCP (The UK Council for Psychotherapy)
A leading organisation for psychotherapists and psychotherapeutic counsellors in the UK.
Includes a national register of UKCP registered psychotherapists.
https://www.psychotherapy.org.uk

NCS (National Counselling Society)
Plays an important role with the profession of counselling in the UK.
Has an accredited register of counsellors.
https://nationalcounsellingsociety.org

NHS
Offers free counselling services on a self-referral as well as GP referral basis.
https://www.nhs.uk

Relate
The UK's largest provider of relationship support, helping people of all ages, backgrounds, sexual orientation and gender identities to strengthen their relationships.
https://relate.org.uk

All you can
change is *yourself,*
but
SOMETIMES
that changes
EVERYTHING

Gary W Goldstein

Printed in Great Britain
by Amazon

13061735R00099